PRESERVED
Fruit

VOLUME 2

PRESERVED

Fruit

DARRA GOLDSTEIN / CORTNEY BURNS / RICHARD MARTIN

PHOTOGRAPHY BY DAVID MALOSH

Hardie Grant

NORTH AMERICA

CONTENTS

RECIPES

In Sweetness and in Health

Preserving fruit began as something pragmatic but has evolved into a dynamic way to create lively, unexpected flavors.

The inherent ephemerality of fruit makes its preservation not so much a means for culinary creativity but a necessity. Short seasonal bursts of flavor and sweetness give way to rot in a matter of days or weeks, which is why, since ancient times, humankind has explored ways to extend the life of its beloved fruits.

As humans have evolved, so have the methods of preserving fruit and enjoying the end product. Early techniques included simply drying fruits in the sun or preserving them in honey, which has a high concentration of sugar. Like salt, sugar prevents contamination. In volume 1 of our Preserved series, *Condiments*, we referred to salt as "the original condiment." It could be said that sugar is the second.

Of course, we now tend to associate sugar with sweetness, but this wasn't always the case, nor was sugar the sole agent—besides the sun— for preserving fruit. In fact, fruit preservation has taken unexpected, playful, and ingenious turns as the practices have developed through-out the ages. Grapes become raisins but also wine; berries transform into jam or fruit leather; apples and pears provide a base for spreads and butters; citrus becomes an agent of change.

In creating the recipes for this volume, we subjected fruits to borderline sadistic experi-ments. We poked holes in apples and soaked them in brine. We peeled and strung persim-mons, suspending them from the rafters. We puréed and then dehydrated cherries (not the only ingredient that insinuated a bloodbath; see Pomegranate Molasses, page 91). So as not to seem entirely inhospitable to our captive fruits, we even allowed a mélange of strawberries, peaches, and pineapples to bathe drunkenly in brandy.

Most of these experiments yielded not just preserved fruits in the ancient tradition but ingredients that can enliven dishes from across many cultures. Cookbooks almost always feature a chapter on cooking with vegetables. Few outside of pastry or baking guides devote much space to employing fruit, whether fresh or preserved.

A purported thirteenth-century Italian proverb states, "Do not let the peasant know how good cheese is with pears." Rather than dissuade you from mixing the sweet with the savory—as the Italians did to prevent workers from eating the fruit rather than picking and packing it—this volume aims to encourage exploration.

These recipes yield jewel-like artifacts to add to your pantry, yes, but they also conjure luxury on a platter alongside fine cheese, or cleverly cut through the fat in grilled meat and game dishes. Some offer straightforward results and pairings; others will surprise and delight. For example, Sicilian Candied Figs (page 33) pair exquisitely with cheese, while the method to prepare them produces a fig syrup that is fantastic in its own right.

Syrups rely on sugar for sweetness, but think back to a time before we associated this viscous concoction with high-fructose corn syrup. The syrups, sauces, and dried fruits featured in the following pages highlight the many benefits of natural sweetness, from health to cultural comingling to reduction of food waste (see our Fruit Scrap Vinegar, page 29, and Spicy Citrus Peel Paste, page 79).

Ounce for ounce, dried fruits are richer in fiber and certain antioxidants than fresh fruit. In Persia and the Caucasus, the practice of making fruit leather dates back centuries, long before Western food-manufacturing conglomerates squeezed out the beneficial ingredients of dried fruit to produce processed "roll-ups." Japanese fruits such as persimmons are known to reduce cholesterol and improve heart health. Sweetness and health, in other words, don't need to be mutually exclusive. The purpose of this book is to have fun with flavor and to globetrot from your own kitchen without sacrificing your well-being.

Preserving fruit may have begun as something functional and pragmatic, but here we offer creative recipes that we hope will bring joy. Included are both serving suggestions and a few additional recipes that call for preserved fruit as an ingredient. The Date Balls with Preserved Lemon Paste (page 46), for instance, make a delectable snack and a great alternative to chocolate or cookies; they are equally at home among bejeweled sweets on a plate with bite-size confections.

The best results may come from happy accidents, as when early Middle Eastern cooks found that a reduction of pomegranate juice drizzled on roasted meats or vegetables creates a mesmerizing dance between sweetness and sharpness. Consider this book a template for new culinary adventures.

Sweet-Tart Apple Butter

Apple butter has an intriguing history. It is thought to date back centuries to orchard-rich monasteries and villages in Belgium and Germany. The practice made its way across the Atlantic with European immigrants, especially German-speaking groups who formed the Pennsylvania Dutch communities. Apple butter later spread throughout Appalachia and the American South. Families regularly turned the production of apple butter into a communal event, producing huge batches of it in large copper kettles. One of America's most well-known brands got its start this way, when a pioneer named Jerome Monroe Smucker purchased an Ohio apple mill in 1897 and began making apple butter over a wood stove. He and his wife ladled the apple butter into crocks to extend the sale of apples year-round, and their apple butter became the foundation for what is now Smucker's jams.

While apple butter isn't as popular today as it once was, we think that our recipe will earn a special place in your larder. Lady apples are first preserved in a brine of sugar, water, vinegar, and spices that adds a depth of flavor to the finished purée, which includes fresh apples. This smooth, tangy spread is irresistible.

2 pounds / 900 g small apples, such as
    Lady apples
2¼ cups / 400 g sucanat
2 cups / 475 ml water
2 cups / 475 ml unseasoned rice vinegar
2 cups / 475 ml white wine vinegar
1 cinnamon stick
3 cloves
10 black peppercorns
1 bay leaf
1½ pounds / 680 g fresh tart apples, such as
    Pink Lady, Honeycrisp, or Cortland

Poke each small apple a few times with a skewer or push pin. Place the apples in a 3-quart / 3 L crock or jar.

In a medium saucepan, bring the sucanat, water, rice vinegar, wine vinegar, cinnamon, cloves, peppercorns, and bay leaf to a boil. Pour the hot brine over the apples and cover the container. Leave them to sit for 1 month in a cool, dark place.

To make the apple butter, drain the pickled apples, reserving the brine. Cut the pickled apples into 1-inch / 2.5 cm slices and place them in a Dutch oven or other large, heavy pot.

Cut the fresh apples into 1-inch / 2.5 cm slices and add them to the pot. Pour in enough of the pickling brine to come halfway up the apples (you will use about half of the reserved brine); discard the rest of the brine.

Cover the apples and brine with a circle of parchment paper (a cartouche) and bring to a boil over medium heat. Cook at a rapid simmer, stirring frequently once the apples begin to soften. Continue cooking until the apples are falling apart and only a shallow layer of liquid remains on the bottom of the pan, about 45 minutes.

Scrape the mixture in batches into a food mill and pass it through the mill to make a very thick, smooth purée. Pack the hot apple butter into small jars, cap them tightly, and refrigerate for up to 4 months. For even longer keeping, see Notes on Canning (page 99).

SERVING SUGGESTIONS FILL THUMBPRINT OR OTHER COOKIES / SPREAD ON BUTTERMILK BISCUITS AND TOP WITH BACON / USE AS A FILLING IN LAYER CAKE WITH MAPLE BUTTERCREAM / ENJOY WITH CHARCUTERIE AND CHEESE

Apple Stack Cake

Grand, multilayered cakes are considered a pinnacle of the professional pastry kitchen—think of Dobos torte with its chocolate buttercream sandwiched between seven layers of sponge cake. Much less well known, and rarely lauded, is apple stack cake, a specialty of the Appalachian region of the southern United States. There, beginning in the nineteenth century, women in the poorest households created towering cakes made largely with the limited ingredients their own households could produce. Apple stack cake was often prepared a few days before laundry day, when women would be too busy to bake but would enjoy a taste of "washday cake." Today, apple stack cake is more often prepared for special occasions, as doing the laundry has become less laborious than baking a multilayered cake.

The secret to this cake is dried apples, which are reconstituted into a purée and then spread between five to seven layers of cake sweetened with sorghum syrup or molasses, both products once readily available on the farm. Lard, also of domestic production, was the original shortening. Some traditional recipes call for pouring batter into a cast-iron skillet and baking the layers one by one; we opt for a quicker method using a cookie-like dough. After assembly, the cake is left to sit for two to three days before serving, giving the apples time to moisten the layers. The result is a richly flavored cake that nearly melts in your mouth.

A few tips are in order for the stack cake to turn out well. Be sure to use brown, naturally dried apples, with no preservatives. The flavor of commercially dried apples isn't nearly as good, and they don't break down easily when cooked; you can also try substituting dried pears. The choice of flour is similarly important. For proper texture, use all-purpose unbleached flour with an 11 percent protein content. A higher protein content will turn the cake crumbly, while cake flour doesn't provide enough structure.

This cake must age for at least two days before serving, so be sure to plan ahead.

FILLING

1 pound / 454 g preservative-free dried apples

Water or unsweetened apple juice (about 6 cups / 1.5 L, enough to barely cover the apples)

1½ firmly packed cups / 330 g light brown sugar

1½ teaspoons ground cinnamon

½ teaspoon ground allspice

Pinch of kosher salt

CAKE LAYERS

½ cup / 113 g unsalted butter, at room temperature

½ cup / 100 g granulated sugar

1 large egg

1 large egg white

½ cup / 120 ml full-fat buttermilk

½ cup / 180 g sorghum syrup

4 cups / 480 g unbleached all-purpose flour

1 teaspoon baking soda

1 teaspoon ground cinnamon

½ teaspoon ground ginger

½ teaspoon grated nutmeg

½ teaspoon kosher salt

Confectioners' sugar, for serving

MAKE THE FILLING: Place the apples in a large saucepan with just enough water to cover. Bring to a boil, then reduce the heat and simmer, uncovered, until the apples are soft and most of the water has evaporated, about 45 minutes. Mash the apples right in the pan with a potato masher (they don't have to be completely smooth, but the filling shouldn't be too chunky). Alternatively, pulse them in a food processor until nearly smooth. Stir in the brown sugar, cinnamon, allspice, and the pinch of salt. Return to the heat and simmer for 5 minutes more, stirring occasionally. Set aside to cool. You will have about 6 cups / 1.3 kg of filling.

MAKE THE CAKE LAYERS: In a medium bowl, cream the butter and sugar until light. In a separate bowl, lightly beat the egg and the egg white with the buttermilk and sorghum syrup until well combined. In a third bowl, mix together the flour, baking soda, cinnamon, ginger, nutmeg, and salt.

Pour about one-third of the buttermilk mixture into the creamed butter, stirring to incorporate it well. Then stir in one-third of the flour mix-ture. Continue to alternate adding the liquid and dry ingredients, stirring well to incorporate them after each addition. The dough will be very soft. Cover the bowl with plastic wrap and chill the dough in the refrigerator for 20 minutes.

Preheat the oven to 375°F / 190°C. Line two large baking sheets with parchment paper.

With floured hands, turn the dough out onto a well-floured surface. Using a bench scraper or knife, divide it into six equal pieces of about 6 ounces / 170 g each. Shape each one into a ball. Place one ball of dough on a prepared baking sheet and pat it out into an 8-inch / 20 cm circle. Don't worry about getting the edges perfect (if you want perfection, you can draw two circles on the parchment as guides). Repeat with a second round. Two rounds should fit on the baking sheet.

Prick each round with a fork, then bake until lightly puffed and just beginning to brown around the edges, 8 to 10 minutes. Let the layers cool on the baking sheet for 5 minutes, then transfer to a rack to finish cooling.

While the first layers are baking, repeat the process with two more pieces of dough. You can bake the last set of rounds on the same parchment paper you used for the first batch.

If the dough has softened too much for easy handling, return it to the refrigerator to chill for 10 minutes.

When the cake layers are cool, set aside the prettiest one to use for the top. Place one layer on a cake plate and spread it with a heaping cup / 225 g of the apple filling to within ½ inch / 1.25 cm of the edge. Continue to stack the cake layers and spread with the apple filling until you have used them all up, ending with the pretty cake layer on top. If the cake tilts to one side, shore up the layers where needed with a little extra filling to even things out.

Store the cake under a dome for 2 days before serving to allow the layers to soften. Just before serving, sprinkle the cake generously with confectioners' sugar. Use a serrated knife to cut the cake into tall slices. It freezes well.

Brined Watermelon

If the only preserved watermelon you've ever tasted is pickled watermelon rind, these wedges of brined watermelon flesh will be a revelation. Where Southern-style pickled rind is heavy on sugar and vinegar, these colorful slices are lacto-fermented in a mild salt solution that is only slightly sweetened with honey, and they're aromatic with herbs and spices. Brined watermelon is a favorite summertime treat in Russia, where whole watermelons are often brined in barrels for long keeping, sometimes with apples added to the brine. The method we use here is much quicker, taking only a few days for the melon to ferment.

Baby watermelons are ideal for ease of preparation, but you can also slice large melons into similarly small wedges. Just be sure to choose a melon that's slightly underripe to ensure that it doesn't turn mushy. Although this vivid pickle makes a great accompaniment to meat, we like it best as an appetizer, especially with a shot of ice-cold vodka.

2 pounds / 900 g baby watermelon

1 ounce / 28 g fresh dill, including seed heads, if possible

2 celery ribs with leaves, cut into 3-inch / 7.5 cm lengths

6 garlic cloves, smashed

8 cups / 2 L water

¼ cup / 36 g kosher salt

¼ cup / 85 g raw, unpasteurized honey

10 black peppercorns

2 whole cloves

1 teaspoon allspice berries

2 bay leaves

Sterilize a 1-gallon / 4 L jar. Rinse the watermelon well and slice into 1-inch / 2.5 cm thick slices, then cut each slice into triangle-shaped wedges. Place some dill in the bottom of the jar, then layer the watermelon with the remaining dill, celery, and garlic. Don't press down on the watermelon.

Next, make the brine. In a medium bowl, mix 2 cups / 475 ml of the water with the salt and honey, stirring until the salt dissolves. Then add the peppercorns, cloves, allspice berries, and bay leaves. Stir in the remaining 6 cups / 1.5 L of water, mixing well. Pour the spiced brine over the melon; it should just cover it. Place a weight on top of the melon to keep it submerged (a plastic zip-top bag filled with water will do the trick). Cover the jar with cheesecloth and secure it with a rubber band. Let the watermelon sit at room temperature for 24 to 48 hours, checking the jar every 12 hours for signs of fermentation. As soon as the brine smells pleasantly sour and small bubbles appear on the surface, it's time to transfer the jar to the refrigerator.

The watermelon will have absorbed a lot of brine and diminished in volume, so at this point, if desired, you can transfer it to a 3-quart / 3 L container. Close tightly with a lid.

The watermelon will be ready to eat as soon as it is well chilled. It will continue to ferment very slowly in the refrigerator, so keep tasting the melon until you find the perfect degree of sourness and effervescence for your taste. The brined watermelon will keep for up to 1 month, though it will become progressively less crisp.

SERVING SUGGESTIONS SERVE WITH GRILLED MEATS / CHOP AND TOSS WITH FRESH WATERMELON, FETA, MINT, AND ONION FOR A REFRESHING SUMMER SALAD / PURÉE INTO VINAIGRETTES TO ADD SOME TANG

Amba

This tangy, bright yellow condiment is a child of the culinary diaspora. Closely related to pickled mango, amba originated in India (the Marathi word āmbā *means "mango"). From there it likely traveled along the Silk Road to Baghdad, although a popular story claims that amba arrived in Iraq only in the nineteenth century, the supposed brainchild of the Baghdadi Sassoon family. Some members of the family had emigrated to Bombay, where they made a fortune in the opium trade. There they also "discovered" mangoes and sent barrels of the fruit to their homeland, pickled in vinegar to endure the transit without spoiling. What's certain is that amba eventually took hold in Iraq in a new form, less as a pickle than as a sauce made by fermenting unripe mangoes, drying them in the sun, then cooking them with aromatic spices, specifically fenugreek.*

Amba continued to travel. In the early 1950s, when more than 100,000 Jews were expelled from Iraq to Israel, they brought a taste for amba with them. The condiment soon entered Israel's culinary repertoire, where it became a favorite accompaniment to street foods such as falafel and sabich, the fried eggplant sandwich in pita. Over the past decade, amba has achieved even broader popularity, thanks to the global rise in Israeli restaurants, though it still retains its Iraqi-Jewish identity.

2 firm, unripe mangoes
1 teaspoon fenugreek seed
¼ teaspoon yellow mustard seed
¼ teaspoon cumin seed
¼ teaspoon ground ginger
¼ teaspoon cayenne pepper
¼ teaspoon smoked paprika
¼ teaspoon ground turmeric
3 tablespoons / 45 ml olive oil
2 garlic cloves, thinly sliced
½ serrano chile (or more, to taste), thinly sliced
1 large lime, zested and juiced

6 PERCENT BRINE
5½ teaspoons kosher salt
1½ cups / 360 ml water

Peel the mangoes and remove the flesh in large slabs from around the pit. Dice the fruit into ¼-inch / 6 mm cubes and transfer to a 1-quart / 1 L glass jar. You will have about 12 ounces / 350 g of fruit.

Make a 6 percent brine by stirring the salt into the water. Pour the brine over the mango to cover it completely, leaving 1¼ to 2 inches / 3 to 5 cm of headspace between the lip of the jar and the brine. Place a weight on top of the mango to keep it submerged (a plastic zip-top bag filled with water will do the trick).

Close the jar tightly and let the mango ferment at room temperature for 10 days. "Burp" the jar a few times a day for the first 5 days to release any pressure that is building up inside the jar. Do this by opening and then retightening the lid.

After 10 days, taste a piece of mango; it should be slightly but not overpoweringly salty, with a nice tang. If not, let the mango ferment a bit longer, tasting each day until it is to your liking. Strain the fruit from the liquid. Set both aside.

To make the amba, finely grind the fenugreek seed, mustard seed, and cumin seed in a spice grinder or mini food processor. Add the ginger, cayenne, smoked paprika, and turmeric and grind again. CONTINUED ▶

In a medium frying pan, heat the oil over medium heat. Add the garlic and chile and cook until the garlic is fragrant and just beginning to color. Add the spices and cook for a minute or so, stirring continuously to make sure the mixture doesn't burn. Stir in the mango, lime zest, and lime juice. Remove from the heat and let cool for 10 minutes.

Purée the mango mixture in a blender or food processor until completely smooth, adding a couple tablespoons of the brine, if necessary, to thin the mixture. Transfer the amba to a glass jar; tap the jar gently on the counter to release any air bubbles. Place a piece of plastic wrap directly against the surface of the purée to protect it from oxygen, and cover the jar with a tight-fitting lid.

Store at room temperature, stirring the amba once a day for 2 to 3 days, covering it well again after each stirring. After 3 days the amba is ready to eat. Keep the jar well sealed with both plastic wrap on the surface and a lid on the jar. Stored this way, the amba will keep for 2 or 3 months in the refrigerator.

SERVING SUGGESTIONS SERVE ALONGSIDE ROASTED CHICKEN, LAMB, OR VEGETABLES / STIR INTO A FRESH SALAD FOR A FRUITY KICK / USE AS A MARINADE FOR FISH / STIR INTO YOGURT TO SERVE WITH FIERY DISHES

Chamoy Sauce

This Mexican chile sauce has a history as complex as its flavor, which is at once fruity, salty, spicy, and sour. The taste is like chile-inflected umeboshi, *the Japanese pickled plums to which the sauce is related. Its first use in Mexico was in* saladitos, *candies made from the dried fruit. In the 1970s, commercial chamoy sauce became a popular street food used to garnish fresh mango slices or flavor popsicles. By the early 1990s chamoy moved into fine restaurants, where it became an object of chefs' desire.*

The origins of the sauce intrigued food historian Rachel Laudan, who has lived in both Mexico and Hawaii, where she found a similar flavor in the snacks known as "crack seed." Rachel discovered that the sauce's name derives from the Cantonese term, see mui, *which eventually morphed into the Spanish chamoy. Chinese workers had introduced the snacks to both Mexico and Hawaii. While crack seed has remained popular in Hawaii, in Mexico chamoy became something entirely new.*

Our recipe calls for dried Angelino plums and apricots for fruitiness, with spices that hint at Tajín, a seasoning made of salt, chile, and lime. Our favorite way to enjoy chamoy sauce is poured over ice cream, but it also adds a thrilling note to savory dishes.

SPICE MIXTURE

1 dried ancho chile, stemmed and seeded

1 dried guajillo chile, stemmed and seeded

2 dried chiles de árbol, stemmed and seeded

1½ teaspoons cumin seed

1½ teaspoons dried oregano

1½ teaspoons garlic powder

½ teaspoon crystallized lime powder, such as True Lime, or black lime powder

½ teaspoon ground coriander

⅛ teaspoon kosher salt

SAUCE

2 cups / 475 ml water

⅔ cup / 80 g dried apricots

½ cup / 65 g dried Angelino plums or apricots

¼ cup / 40 g raisins

¼ cup / 7 g dried hibiscus flowers

3 to 4 dried chiles de árbol, seeded

2 tablespoons / 24 g sucanat or brown sugar

2 tablespoons / 30 ml freshly squeezed lime juice

⅛ teaspoon kosher salt

PREPARE THE SPICE MIXTURE: Tear the chiles and place them in a small skillet with the cumin seed. Toast over medium heat until fragrant, 3 to 4 minutes. Be careful not to burn. Remove from the heat and let cool.

Transfer the toasted chiles and cumin to a spice grinder or mini food processor and grind into a powder. Add the oregano, garlic powder, crystallized lime powder, ground coriander, and salt. Grind and set aside. Any leftover spice mixture can be kept in an airtight jar and stored at room temperature up to 6 months.

PREPARE THE SAUCE: In a small saucepan, combine the water, dried apricots, dried plums, raisins, hibiscus, and chiles de árbol and bring to a boil. Simmer, covered, until the fruit is plump, about 15 minutes. Let cool for 15 minutes, then transfer to a blender along with 1½ tablespoons of the spice mixture, the sucanat, lime juice, and salt. Blend until smooth.

Store in the refrigerator for up to 6 months.

SERVING SUGGESTIONS USE IN PALETAS (MEXICAN ICE POPS) / SHAKE INTO MEZCAL COCKTAILS / SPLASH OVER FRESH FRUIT OR CRISP VEGETABLES LIKE CUCUMBERS AND JICAMA

Red Currant and Juniper "Cheese"

Fruit butters and cheeses live an independent life, entirely unconnected to dairy: these words describe fruits that have been preserved with sugar. Butters are fruit cooked down to a spreadable consistency, like apple butter, while fruit cheese is firm enough to slice with a knife. For fruit cheese, high-pectin fruits are required. To achieve an appealing tartness, we make ours with red or black currants. And although fruit cheese is most often formed into a loaf or a slab, we choose to make ours in small, decorative molds that yield single servings just right for snacking, or for taking an honored place on a cheese board. Unlike the more delicate French jellies known as pâtes de fruits, *fruit cheeses can be held for months in the refrigerator, where they retain their beautiful gloss.*

2 pounds / 900 g red or black currants, fresh or frozen (weighed after they've been stemmed)

1 tablespoon juniper berries or anise seed, finely ground

About 3 cups / 750 ml water

1½ cups / 300 g granulated sugar

3 tablespoons / 45 ml freshly squeezed lemon juice

Combine the currants and the ground juniper in a heavy pot and add enough water to just barely cover the fruit. Bring the mixture to a boil over medium heat, then simmer for 30 minutes, or until the currants burst easily when gently pressed against the side of the pot. Remove the pan from the heat and crush the fruit slightly with an immersion blender.

Place a sieve over a large bowl and drain the mixture, pressing down hard to extract as much juice as possible. You'll be left with only a small amount of pulp in the sieve, which you can discard.

Prepare small baking molds, such as miniature tartlet pans, silicone molds, or cannelé molds, by brushing them with a neutral vegetable oil, such as grapeseed. Set the molds on a cookie sheet.

Return the strained liquid to the pan along with the sugar and lemon juice. Bring to a full boil and cook over medium heat for another 30 to 40 minutes, watching the mixture closely toward the end to make sure it doesn't scorch. Continue reducing it until you have a very thick jam; you should be able to draw a line with a spoon along the bottom of the pot that will slowly fill back in.

Preheat the oven to 175°F / 80°C. While the jam is still hot, spoon it into the prepared molds. Place them in the oven and warm them for 15 to 20 minutes, until the surface of the jellies feels firm to the touch. Remove from the oven and let cool completely before using an offset spatula to release them from the molds. Fruit cheese will keep in an airtight container in the refrigerator for up to 6 months.

SERVING SUGGESTIONS SERVE ON A CHEESE PLATE / STIR INTO BONE BROTH TO MAKE A SAUCE FOR GAME / LAYER INTO A GRILLED CHEESE SANDWICH

JUNE TAYLOR

June Taylor is revered for the fruit preserves and confectionery she produced at The Still-Room in Berkeley, California, before closing the shop in 2021.

What makes your fruit preserves distinctive?
They are intense in flavor, very fruit-forward. That's partly the result of a decision I made thirty years ago to reject the high sugar content in preserve making. I also follow a traditional methodology that is intimate, very detailed, and without the use of commercial pectin. In my entire career, I've never made anything with commercial pectin.

I've been fortunate to study antiquarian confectionery and preserving books, British books, both in the British Library and in private collections. They have taught me a lot about preserving, and I've brought that knowledge and that sensibility to my own work.

I created a kitchen garden over two decades ago to grow herbs and flowers. So I bring into my preserving work an appreciation of how plants can enhance and complement fruit. I also explore rare and forgotten fruits. That's been in the mix for me in terms of a desire to support family farmers. If we don't support our local community, we will lose them. We've lost a lot of orchards to the monolithic grape.

The preserve-making work that I do is not just about making a product. When you look at the shelves of preserves in grocery stores, they've diminished to a handful of fruits, generic fruits. I've worked hard and long to bring awareness and appreciation of fruits that have become rare and almost extinct.

You make marmalades, conserves, syrups, chutneys, ketchups, candied citrus peels, and more. Can you tell us how you decide which product is best for a particular ingredient?

There's a natural affinity of a fruit to a process. I don't believe that there's such a thing as blueberry marmalade. I also believe in a no-waste approach. If I got in Meyer lemons, for example, and the farmer, bless him, had given me teeny tiny fruit, I would say to myself, okay, I'm going to salt cure them. My candy making came out of the fact that I was composting so much of my citrus peel. I don't support commercial agriculture and the use of pesticides and fungicides in our food, so I'm comfortable with candying the excess peel. I taught myself over a period of about four years to understand the intricacies of confectionery work, which is challenging. Marmalade and confectionery work are a lot more challenging than basic conserves.

I think about flavor, the structure of the fruit, the season. Learning about the characteristics of the fruit enables you to decide how to preserve it.

How would you describe your use of aromatics, and how do you go about pairing different flavors?
I built a kitchen garden at my home, and I grow a variety of fruit. I have a yuzu tree. I have a Satsuma plum tree. I have an apple tree. But you know, over twenty-five years ago, farmers weren't growing herbs and flowers in the way that they are now, even here in Northern California in the local farmers' markets. You couldn't get bunches of lavender or rose geranium. So, I started to grow them myself. And as a close observer of nature, I look at the seasonality of plants and fruit.

I think about complementation or contrast. It's exciting and challenging as a preserve maker to complement, enhance, or contrast a fruit to bring another layer of appreciation. It became fun for me to do not just one infusion, but two. For example, I'm probably going to play with Meyer lemons and bay and rose together. This was something that I did a lot of in my herbal infusions. I was asked to produce an aperitif syrup for a Sicilian meal. So, I was really interested in working with rosemary and white sage and bringing two savory flavors together, one of which has a sweeter element. It's playful. It's challenging.

Aromatics are another element of nature that I'm bringing into my work; it's not unknown in the British tradition. I am British, and I believe that we are a great preserving nation. We have a fantastic history. All the stereotypes about British food are most often contemporary and without an appreciation of what's been done in the past. I've always wanted to honor history and learn from it and bring it into a modern focus. I think if you would sum up my work, it's tradition with a very modern focus.

How do you decide what to do with a specific ingredient, such as bay?

Bay's kind of become hip, you know, but I've been doing this for so many years, and I've seen slowly how things come into focus. I'm looking at my yuzu tree out in my garden. It's been in the ground for fifteen or twenty years, and until recently it was pretty much unknown outside of Japan. But now yuzu is very well-known and appreciated. I had a Mediterranean bay tree that grew so big that I had to take it out, but the stump still sprouts bay leaves. I adore bay laurel and we have it growing here in plentitude, so I also forage. One of my most popular combinations is yuzu and bay laurel. Mostly I did it

as a syrup for drinks, vinaigrettes, marinades, and drizzle-over, but I also did it as a candy, as a confection. It spoke to people.

It's not difficult for me to imagine flavors together. What is difficult is to have the opportunity to make as many preserves as my ideas generate. When I had The Still-Room, not all of my ideas were successful, because when one works with fruits that are unknown, there's only a small proportion of people who will be inspired to try them. The marketplace is relatively conservative. So, twenty years ago, I was making blood orange slices in a clementine syrup. They were beautiful, but they never sold. The marketplace exists.

Do you have any advice for people who are eager to try their hand at preserving fruits?

Go for it. Don't be scared. You're not going to harm anyone making jam. I'm older but I think about the generations who have been raised on industrial food. My work harkens back to the pre-industrial in style, scale, attention, and understanding, but I'm a modern person with a modern interpretation. I want to encourage new generations to keep going with that. Let's take the skill back from industry. Let's make it normal again to make one's own preserves.

Silver Lime and Blue Tuscan Rosemary Jelly

This jelly is crystal clear with suspended pieces of lime peel. Similar to a marmalade, it is a juice-based citrus preserve. Silver limes, a seedless Bearss lime known also as Persian or Tahitian limes, are yellow, thin-skinned, juicy, and a perfect fruit for jelly making. This recipe relies on a naturally derived pectin which enables a better set for the jelly.

2½ pounds / 1 kg organic silver limes (to yield
    2½ cups / 600 ml lime juice), and 1 cup /
    100 g lime peel
10 cups water
5 cups / 1 kg organic sugar
7 tablespoons / 12 g fresh rosemary, such as
    Blue Tuscan

Rinse the fruit and cut in half. Juice the fruit and strain the juice through a fine-mesh strainer to remove any pulp.

Use a small sharp knife to remove the loose membranes inside the shells. Cut the shells into thin, even-sized julienned pieces. Reserve all the membranes and any lime solids from juicing to make the pectin.

Combine the juice, peel, and water in a pot. Place the membranes in a small cotton jelly bag and suspend in the pot.

Bring the mixture to a boil, then reduce the heat to a steady simmer, and cook until the peel is tender and offers no resistance when chewed, approximately 16 minutes. Remove the jelly bag and cool.

Add 4⅓ cups /866 g of the sugar to the mixture and stir to dissolve. Reserve the remainder to use later if needed. Taste to check the sweetness of the liquid for the desired balance between sweetness and acid.

When the pectin bag is cool, gently squeeze the bag to release the pectin and add to the jelly mixture.

Divide the mixture into two smaller pots, approximately 6 cups /½ g in each. Divide the rosemary into two cotton jelly bags, tying one to each pot handle and suspending them in the mixture.

Bring each pot to a rolling boil and cook for 10 minutes. Stir the jelly occasionally to ensure even cooking.

Place clean, dry jars in a 225°F /107°C oven for 10 minutes prior to jarring the jelly to heat them up.

After 10 minutes, taste the jelly, and if the rosemary flavor is clear and pronounced remove the jelly bag. If not, leave it in the jelly as it continues to cook. Check the sweetness of the jelly, and if necessary, add more sugar to taste.

Continue cooking for approximately 10 minutes and check the consistency of the jelly by placing a very small amount on a plate, letting it cool, and running a finger across the surface. If it crinkles, a set has been achieved. Longer cooking will result in a firmer set.

When a set has been reached, taste the jelly and make any final adjustments with added sugar or a little lime juice to create a satisfying balance.

Combine the two pots and skim off any surface scum on the jelly.

Remove the jars from the oven and place on a cooling rack. Quickly fill them to within ⅛ inch / 3 mm of the rim. If any drops land on the rim, wipe with a clean, wet cloth. Place lids on the jars and screw tight. Leave to cool on the rack, undisturbed, until a vacuum seal has been reached.

Fruit Scrap Vinegar

Fruit scrap vinegar is a no-waste solution to preserving the otherwise-discarded parts of fruit. The fermentation crock will turn your kitchen into a fizzy mini-laboratory, doubling as a conversation piece.

Start by saving cores, peels, and any fruit scraps in the freezer until you have at least 1 pound/454 g. We like to use apples, pears, quince, and persimmons; avoid highly acidic fruits like pineapple. The scraps are fermented with honey, and then vinegar, over a period of three weeks. The strained vinegar continues to ferment for at least two months. It's important to taste it regularly. Fermented vinegar reaches a point when the acid is perfectly balanced; after achieving that peak, the flavor can begin to decline. The length of time it takes depends on variables like room temperature.

The reward for months of waiting is a fruity vinegar that will enliven any number of dishes. This recipe can easily be scaled to larger amounts.

4 tablespoons fermented honey or raw, unpasteurized honey
4 cups/950 ml warm water
1 pound/454 g fruit scraps, peels, and cores
½ cup raw, unfiltered apple cider vinegar

In a 2-quart/2 L wide-mouth canning jar or crock, stir the honey into the water. Once the honey is dissolved, add the fruit scraps. To keep fruit flies out, cover tightly with cheese-cloth, and secure it with the jar's ring or with rubber bands. Let the mixture stand at warm room temperature (72° to 80°F/22° to 27°C) for 5 to 10 days, until it begins to ferment and taste tangy and slightly alcoholic. Stir in the vinegar, replace the cheesecloth, and let sit for 2 weeks, stirring once a day for the first 5 days to oxygenate the mixture; secure the cheese-cloth after each stir. At this point you should see bubbles, indicating active fermentation.

After 2 weeks, strain the solids. Avoid decanting any thick yeast that may have settled at the bottom. Clean the container and pour in the strained liquid; the container should be about three-quarters full. Cover once again with cheesecloth. Let stand in a dark spot at warm room temperature (72° to 80°F/22° to 27°C), for 2 to 4 months, tasting every week or so until the vinegar is acidified to your liking.

When it tastes right to you, strain the vinegar into narrow-neck bottles and cap tightly. Continue to age it at room temperature to mellow the acidity for 6 months or so before using. The vinegar will keep indefinitely at room temperature.

FRUIT SCRAP VINEGAR SYRUP
MAKES ABOUT 2 CUPS / 475 ML

Should you crave something sweet, follow the recipe below to turn the vinegar into a lovely syrup.

2 cups/475 ml Fruit Scrap Vinegar
2 packed cups/400 g light brown sugar

Combine the vinegar and brown sugar in a heavy saucepan and bring to a boil over medium heat, stirring until the sugar dissolves. Lower the heat and simmer for 15 to 20 minutes, until the mixture is syrupy and has reduced by about 25 percent. The syrup will keep indefinitely in the refrigerator.

SERVING SUGGESTIONS SPOON OVER ICE CREAM / USE TO MAKE POPSICLES / ADD TO COCKTAILS

Blueberries in the Style of Capers

One of summer's great pleasures is a bowl of ripe blueberries, juicy and sweet. But their season is all too fleeting. This recipe reveals an entirely different side to the fruit, one that can be enjoyed when fresh berries have disappeared. Picked when still green and allowed to ferment for a couple of weeks, blueberries transform from a sweet fruit into a tangy pickle, with lovely herbal notes that explode in the mouth. They're a surefire conversation starter as people try to guess what they are, especially when they're highlighted on a cheese board. Or, for a puckery change, use them instead of capers in sauces or salads.

1 cup / 125 g green, unripe blueberries
1 cup / 240 ml water
1 tablespoon kosher salt

Wash the blueberries thoroughly to remove any dirt and place them in a nonreactive 1-pint / 475 ml glass jar or fermentation crock. In a small bowl, stir together the water and salt until the salt has dissolved. Pour over the berries and mix well.

Place a piece of plastic wrap directly on the surface of the berries to keep them submerged in the brine; if you have a fermentation weight, this is a good time to use it. Seal the container, using a lid with an airlock if you have one; if you don't, open the container every few days to release the carbon dioxide buildup and check for mold. Place the container in a clean, low-light area with a temperature of 60° to 68°F / 16° to 20°C and leave until the berries taste tart and sour, 10 to 14 days.

Store the brined berries in the refrigerator, where they will keep for at least 6 months. Their flavor continues to improve as they age.

SERVING SUGGESTIONS CHOP INTO BUTTER SAUCES FOR FISH DISHES / USE IN BEEF TARTARE / ADD TO VINAIGRETTES / CHOP INTO REMOULADE OR INTO SALSA VERDE IN PLACE OF CAPERS

Sicilian Candied Figs

Sicily may be renowned as the birthplace of the Mafia, but among its contributions there exists something far sweeter and more enduring to the Western world: the art of making confectionery. When Saracens invaded the island in the ninth century, they introduced sugarcane, along with the techniques used to refine it. Over the course of several centuries Sicilians developed not only an important sugar industry but also the ability to work the refined cane into extraordinary confections. As these methods spread throughout Europe, they revolutionized the world of sweets.

Sugar can transform fresh fruit into shimmering, jewel-like candies, while also preserving it. But candying is a laborious process, involving repeated macerations in several batches of increasingly concentrated sugar syrup, until the fruit is thoroughly saturated, which ensures its long keeping. Some traditional recipes called for forty days of processing to achieve the perfect texture; happily, our recipe calls for a mere four.

Figs are native to the western Mediterranean, including Sicily, where they thrive in Mount Etna's rich volcanic soil. They are one of our favorite fruits to candy since they can be preserved whole, retaining their charming shape. As the sugar syrup cooks down, it begins to caramelize, so the flavor of the finished fruit has an ever so slightly bitter note that balances its overall sweetness.

3 cups / 700 ml water
3 cups / 700 ml freshly squeezed lemon juice
Scant 7½ cups / 1.5 kg sugar, plus more for
     coating
1 pound / 454 g fresh figs

In a large, heavy pot, bring the water, lemon juice, and sugar to a slow simmer, stirring to dissolve the sugar. Add the figs and cover them with a circle of parchment paper (a cartouche) to hold them in place. Simmer slowly for 1 hour. Remove the pot from the heat, cover with a lid, and leave at room temperature for 24 hours.

Repeat this process three more times. If the syrup reduces too much, make a small amount in the same ratio (1 cup water, 1 cup lemon juice, and 2½ cups sugar) and add it to the figs so that they have plenty of room to bob around. Once the syrup has cooled for the last time, gently lift out the figs with a slotted spoon and set them on a wire rack to drain. The syrup can be refrigerated and used for cocktails or in cooking.

Place the figs in a dehydrator set to 105°F / 40°C and dry them for 36 hours, until they are tacky and somewhat firm but not completely dehydrated. Cool to room temperature.

Pour a couple of inches of sugar into a bowl and toss the candied figs in the sugar, coating them well. Wrap each fig individually in parchment paper and place in an airtight container. They will keep in the refrigerator for 1 year.

SERVING SUGGESTIONS SERVE WITH SLICED CURED MEATS / DICE AND SAUTÉ WITH ONIONS TO SERVE WITH GAME MEATS / SLICE AND LAYER INTO BRIE EN CROÛTE / DICE AND MIX INTO MUFFIN BATTER

Fermented Honey Charoset

Charoset, a mandatory component of the Passover seder plate, is a fruit and nut mixture that symbolizes the mortar that the ancient Israelites used to make bricks during their years of labor in Egypt. It is eaten with maror—*bitter herbs that represent the harshness of exile. Charoset's sweetness serves to soften that bite.*

Although charoset is a universal food of the Jewish diaspora, it has many regional variations. Most familiar to Americans is the Ashkenazic style of charoset, which hails from Eastern Europe and contains apples, honey, cinnamon, wine, and walnuts or almonds. It is often chunky, in contrast to Sephardic-style charoset, which contains binding ingredients like dates and raisins and dried figs that are easily blended into a paste. Other versions reflect even more local tastes: Italians often add chestnuts, while the Jews of Curaçao prepare garosa, *a mixture of dates, figs, raisins, peanuts, cashews, and brown sugar shaped into balls.*

Our version begins with apples in the Ashkenazic style, but we depart from tradition by adding dried fruits along with aromatics like ginger, cardamom, and orange blossom water. If you want to turn this charoset into a Sephardic-style paste, simply pulse the mixture in a food processor once you have strained it. You don't need a Jewish holiday to celebrate charoset in any form—we enjoy it year-round.

1 pound / 454 g raw, unpasteurized honey

1 cinnamon stick

3 whole cloves

10 ounces / 284 g tart apples, such as Granny Smith or Pink Lady, cored and cut into ¼-inch / 6 mm dice

½ cup / 85 g dried tart cherries, halved or quartered

½ cup / 75 g dried apricots, cut into ¼-inch / 6 mm dice

½ cup / 75 g golden raisins (halved if unusually large)

2-inch knob / 13 g fresh ginger, peeled and finely grated

2 tablespoons / 30 ml red wine or pomegranate juice

1 tablespoon orange blossom water

¼ teaspoon ground cardamom

1¼ cups / 113 g walnuts, pistachios, or almonds, toasted and chopped

Coarse salt for finishing

Place 8 ounces / 227 g of the honey in a 2-quart / 2 L jar along with the cinnamon stick and cloves.

In a large bowl, combine the diced apples, dried cherries, dried apricots, golden raisins, and grated ginger. Stir in the wine, orange blossom water, and ground cardamom. Add to the jar with the honey. Pour the remaining 8 ounces / 227 g of honey over the fruit. Cover the jar with a tight-fitting lid and leave to ferment at room temperature (68° to 72°F / 20° to 22°C).

The fermentation steps take time but require little effort. Over the first few hours you will see the honey begin to seep around the fruit. Let the mixture sit overnight. The next morning, give the mixture a gentle stir and cover the jar tightly again. During the next few days, the mixture will begin to bubble. Once it is quite liquid, gently shake the jar every day, being careful to keep the fruit intact. After 1 week, begin tasting the mixture until it has reached the flavor and texture you like. We prefer ours after about 4 weeks, but feel free to ferment it longer; since honey is a preservative, the fruit remains safe at room temperature for months. Once the fruit has fermented to your liking, place it in the refrigerator.

When you are ready to serve the charoset, remove the jar from the refrigerator the night before to make straining easier. Scrape the fruit into a fine-mesh sieve and allow it to drain over a bowl for several hours, covered with a kitchen towel to discourage any bugs.

To serve, add the toasted and chopped nuts to the fruit and sprinkle with a bit of coarse salt over the top.

SERVING SUGGESTIONS   DOLLOP ON GRANOLA / SERVE ALONGSIDE GRILLED GAME BIRDS / USE UNSTRAINED OVER ICE CREAM OR CREPES / STIR INTO YOGURT / MAKE A CHAROSET CHUTNEY BY MIXING IN CHOPPED FRESH CILANTRO AND MINT

Hoshigaki

Hoshigaki, *as these fruits are called in Japan, are made in late fall by peeling unripe Hachiya persimmons and hanging them to air-dry until the surface develops a sugary white bloom. As they dry, the persimmons are gently massaged to help bring the natural sugars to the surface—a technique we find soothing, just as we find the very presence of the dangling orange orbs cheering. When they're completely dry, the persimmons are sliced and often served with green tea, whose bitterness offers a lovely counterpoint to the fruit. In Japan, hoshigaki are eaten at the New Year to augur good fortune.*

When selecting persimmons to dry, don't be tempted to substitute the sweeter variety of Fuyu persimmons, which are often more readily available, as they are too soft for the drying process and tend to mold. Also be sure to look for persimmons that still have at least an inch of stem so there's something to attach the twine to. (Some online sources sell Hachiya persimmons with T-shaped stems that make for easy hanging.) And finally, if you want to take an extra step to keep mold from forming, spray the persimmons with a little vodka once you have hung them.

Very firm, unripe Hachiya persimmons

Choose any number of persimmons, preferably with stems attached. If it happens that your persimmons don't have stems, you can carefully screw a sterilized eye hook into the top of each fruit. Use a sharp paring knife to trim the peel from the top by carefully slicing from the outside of each persimmon toward the stem, turning the fruit as you go to score all the way around the top. Make a slit in the loosened peel to pull it from the fruit, making sure to leave the stem intact. Remove the remaining peel from each fruit; they will be a bit slippery to work with. Then securely knot a length of twine to each stem.

For drying, choose a fairly cool, well-ventilated space where the persimmons can hang without being disturbed; the temperature should be no warmer than 65°F / 18°C. After 3 to 5 days, once the surfaces of the fruits have become slightly dry, gently massage each fruit to begin coaxing the sugars to the surface and to press out any air pockets where mold could form. Repeat this gentle massage every 3 days for 4 to 6 weeks, until the surface is coated with a white, sugary bloom and the fruit feels leathery. (Even if no bloom has appeared, when the texture feels right, proceed as directed below; the bloom will surface once the persimmons are stored airtight.)

Remove the persimmons from the twine and set them on a cutting board. With a rolling pin, gently roll the fruits flat to eliminate any air pockets. Place the hoshigaki in an airtight container and store in a cool, dark place. They will keep for 6 months.

SERVING SUGGESTIONS SLICE AND SERVE AS PART OF AN AFTER-DINNER CONFECTION PLATTER / EAT AS A TRAIL SNACK / SERVE WITH A CUP OF CHEONG HONEY TEA (PAGE 95)

Lemon Butter-Stuffed Hoshigaki

Japanese wagashi *shops offer a wonderland of beautifully displayed confections. Among them you're likely to find artistic renditions of seasonal fruits and nuts, many of which appear almost too stunning to eat. Here we honor that culinary tradition by dressing up another Japanese delicacy,* hoshigaki, *dried persimmons, with a luscious filling of preserved lemon butter, then slicing the fruit into elegant strips. Hoshigaki are so delicious on their own that it's hardly necessary to adorn them, but once you've had a bite of chewy persimmons paired with creamy, salty-sweet butter, we're sure you'll agree that the combination is divine, worthy of a spot among more traditional jewel-like* wagashi.

1 cup / 225 g unsalted cultured butter, at room temperature
½ teaspoon grated lemon zest
2 tablespoons / 35 g preserved lemon paste, homemade (page 43) or store bought
12 to 16 Hoshigaki (page 38)

In a medium bowl, using a hand-held mixer, cream the butter until light and fluffy, then stir in the lemon zest and the preserved lemon paste. Set aside.

Line a small baking sheet with parchment paper. Place the hoshigaki on a cutting board and cut off the stem end. Then make a slice down the side of each hoshigaki, cutting through almost, but not quite, to the other side. Open the hoshigaki like a book.

Scoop 1 to 2 tablespoons of the butter into the cavity and gently fold the top half over it, pressing lightly to make an even layer inside the fruit. With the back of a spoon or an offset spatula, scrape any excess butter from the edges, smoothing it to create a tidy package.

As you finish filling each one, place it on the prepared baking sheet. Once all are ready, place the baking sheet in the refrigerator for at least 1 hour to firm up the butter.

To serve, remove the hoshigaki from the refrigerator and cut into ½-inch / 1.25 cm slices. Store in an airtight container in the refrigerator, where they will keep for 2 weeks.

Preserved Lemons

When life gives you lemons, you don't have to sweeten it by making lemonade. Instead of adding sugar, put the lemons to use by preserving them in salt. The core ingredient here is really patience, since the lemons take time to soften, but once they do, they will keep for up to a year. Preserved lemons are a wonderfully versatile ingredient to have on hand, adding brightness and depth to a Moroccan tagine or to any kind of stew or braised meat. We especially like to turn preserved lemons into a silken paste with a slightly salty edge, which can be used in savory and sweet dishes alike (see the recipes for Lemon Butter–Stuffed Hoshigaki, page 41, and for Date Balls with Preserved Lemon Paste, page 46).

3½ pounds / 1.6 kg lemons
½ cup / 72 g kosher salt
Freshly squeezed lemon juice (optional)

Juice 2½ pounds / 1.2 kg of the lemons. Strain the juice through a fine-mesh sieve and set it aside. You should have about 2¼ cups / 550 ml of juice.

Wash the remaining 1 pound / 454 g of lemons and remove any stems. Starting at the stem end, cut each fruit into four wedges with a paring knife, cutting down to, but not through, the base, so that each lemon stays intact. Holding a lemon over a bowl, gently pry the quarters apart, then press salt against all of the cut surfaces, capturing any excess salt in the bowl. Repeat with the remaining lemons.

Pack the salted lemons, along with any extra salt, into a sterilized 1-quart / 1 L jar. Pour in the reserved lemon juice to cover the fruit completely. Close the jar tightly and place it in a clean, low-light area at a temperature of 60° to 68°F / 16° to 20°C for 3 to 4 weeks, turning the jar upside down occasionally to prevent the growth of mold. Add a little more lemon juice, if needed, to keep the lemons submerged. The lemons are ready when the peels look slightly translucent, though they taste best when left to mature for 3 months before using. Transfer the jar to the refrigerator, where the lemons will keep for over a year.

SERVING SUGGESTIONS PURÉE INTO SALAD DRESSINGS / CHOP INTO OLIVE MARINADES / SLICE INTO BRAISES / DICE THE RIND INTO SAUCES / USE THE LIQUID IN COCKTAILS

PRESERVED LEMON PASTE

2 cups / 212 g Preserved Lemons (opposite)
¼ cup / 60 ml reserved brine from Preserved
  Lemons
¼ cup / 60 ml freshly squeezed lemon juice

Drain the lemons, reserving the brine. Remove the seeds from the lemons and place the lemons in a blender with the brine and the fresh lemon juice. Purée until smooth.

Pour the mixture into a 9 by 13-inch / 24 by 36 cm glass baking dish, so that the paste is no more than 2 inches / 5 cm deep. Dehydrate at 125°F / 52°C for about 3 hours, until the lemon paste is as thick as tomato paste, giving it a quick stir after 2 hours. If you don't have a dehydrator, you can partially cover the dish and bake the paste at 170°F / 77°C for 3 to 6 hours, stirring every 30 minutes, until it has thickened.

Scrape the paste into a blender and purée it once more, until perfectly smooth. Pack into an airtight container. The paste will keep indefinitely in the refrigerator.

SERVING SUGGESTIONS MAKE PRESERVED LEMON BUTTER (PAGE 41) / PURÉE INTO VINAIGRETTES / USE IN MARINADES FOR FISH / PURÉE AND STIR INTO COCKTAILS FOR A BURST OF ACIDITY AND SALINITY

Date Balls with Preserved Lemon Paste

This recipe summons the taste of Morocco, a country known for two of the recipe's key ingredients: Medjool dates and preserved lemons, which together yield a heavenly salty-sweet confection, perfect for snacking or gracing a dessert plate. The Middle Eastern flavor is amplified by the addition of tahini and sesame seeds, which add a nice crunch to the soft dates and filling.

¾ cup / 170 g unsalted butter

1¼ cups / 225 g pitted Medjool dates

3 tablespoons / 45 ml freshly squeezed lemon juice

4½ teaspoons tahini

½ teaspoon ground cardamom

½ teaspoon ground ginger

½ teaspoon kosher salt

¼ cup / 70 g preserved lemon paste, homemade (page 43) or store bought

Toasted black and/or white sesame seeds for rolling

Preheat the oven to 200°F / 95°C.

Combine 6 tablespoons / 85 g of the butter in a small, ovenproof saucepan with the dates, lemon juice, tahini, cardamom, ginger, and salt (no need to stir them together). Cover the saucepan and bake the mixture until the dates are very soft, 45 minutes to 1 hour. Cool to room temperature.

To finish the date balls, first bring the remaining 6 tablespoons / 85 g butter to room temperature. Use a food processor to purée the date mixture, softened butter, and preserved lemon paste until smooth and emulsified. Refrigerate, covered, until thoroughly chilled before rolling the balls, about 1 hour.

Put the toasted sesame seeds in a bowl. Use a small scoop or spoon to portion the date mixture into balls of about 2 teaspoons each. Roll them in the sesame seeds until they are coated. Allow the balls to chill for an hour before serving. They can be refrigerated in an airtight container for up to 3 weeks.

CHURCHKHELA

Deep in the Caucasus, in the country of Georgia, grapes are revered. *Vitis vinifera*—the original wine grape—is native to the region, where winemaking has been practiced for eight thousand years. Even Georgia's acceptance of Christianity is tied to the grape: when Saint Nino of Capadoccia arrived in the fourth century, she carried a cross made from plaited vines tied with her own hair, ostensibly a symbol of a divine endorsement of winemaking. Grapes also find their way into Georgian cuisine. One of the country's most iconic foods, churchkhela, consists of strands of walnuts or hazelnuts that have been dipped into thickened grape juice to form colorful, sausage-shaped snacks.

Numerous origin stories swirl around churchkhela. An unlikely one tells of a young boy in a monastery kitchen who accidentally dropped his rosary into a kettle of grape juice that he was boiling to make a celebratory porridge. His superior became so enraged that he ordered the boy to eat the rosary. The boy dutifully hung the hot, dripping beads from a tree and left them to cool. When he returned to endure his punishment, he found the thickened juice very much to his liking and urged his superior to taste it. The monk agreed that the boy had stumbled upon a useful coating for nuts, and henceforth the monastery prepared churchkhela for every holiday. Another legend links the preparation to the eleventh-century reign of King David IV (the Builder), who was engaged in numerous wars and needed a ready supply of portable, high-energy food—an early gorp—for his soldiers to carry into battle. While the first story ties churchkhela to the sacred, the second validates it through association with a legendary figure.

The truth is that no one really knows where churchkhela originated, especially since other countries, including Turkey, Armenia, and

Greece, enjoy a similar food. But laying claim to churchkhela is particularly important to Georgia's national identity. Three years after Russia invaded and annexed parts of Georgia in 2008, the Georgians filed for trademark protection to legally brand a number of foods as certifiably Georgian, a patent that the Russians refused to honor. In addition to churchkhela, these include the famous cheese bread khachapuri, chacha (a potent grape-pomace brandy), and several Georgian cheeses.

Churchkhela's popularity is visible throughout Georgia. City markets and roadside stands alike display bright strands of nuts in a multitude of colors derived from the specific variety of grapes that were pressed. The most widespread red wine grape in Georgia is saperavi. Most red grapes have white interiors, but saperavi is ink-black throughout (the word means "dye") and yields gorgeous burgundy juice, thanks to the anthocyanin in the pulp, which incidentally is also a good source of antioxidants. White grape varieties such as rkatsiteli or mtsvane produce pale golden to amber strands. Other colors—from purple to bright red to ruby—can be achieved by using mulberry juice (common in western Georgia), as well as the juice from pomegranates, cherries, apricots, and plums. There are even churchkhelas in neon lime, yellow, and orange, the result of artificial dyes.

Churchkhela is traditionally made during the fall wine harvest. The process is slow, but when performed communally it becomes a joyous occasion. The first step is to ready the strands by leaving the strung nuts to dry in the sun for a few days. Next, the freshly pressed grape juice is boiled down into a concentrate called *badagi*. Once it has thickened, the badagi is mixed with wheat flour (or, in western Georgia, with fine cornmeal) and cooked into a very thick mixture called *tatara*, into which the strands of nuts are dipped. After the strands dry slightly, the process of dipping and drying the nuts is repeated several times until the nuts are well coated. The most traditional method of dipping—described in the Slow Food Foundation's Ark of Taste—is carried out in large cauldrons over a wood fire, which lends a subtle, slightly smoky taste to the grape coating. The finished strands are hung until the coating is completely dry.

Although churchkhela can be eaten right away, it is usually aged for a few months after the harvest to be enjoyed as a New Year's treat. As the confection ages, the coating becomes ever firmer and takes on a white bloom from sugar rising to the surface. When sliced, the nuts are revealed in a beautiful pattern.

Churchkhela

The tongue-twisting name churchkhela *comes from a root meaning "skeleton," lending a vivid image of skeletons dangling on threads awaiting the juice that will coat them. But there's nothing ghoulish about these long strands of grape juice–coated nuts. Bursting with nourishment, they are Georgia's answer to energy bars. During the grape harvest in Georgia—the ancient home of winemaking in the Caucasus Mountains—street stalls are bedecked with churchkhela in a rainbow of colors from royal purple to orange and gold, depending on the type of grape used. Making churchkhela at home isn't hard, but it does involve a series of repetitions, so think of it as a creative project.*

Because some of the walnut halves will inevitably break when you thread them, it's a good idea to toast a few more than the recipe calls for. The strands of churchkhela can be eaten shortly after they are dry, although Georgians usually store them, wrapped in clean kitchen towels, until the winter holidays, to offer a sweet start to the new year. By this time churchkhela often develops a harmless white bloom as sugar rises to the surface. To eat the confection, simply pull the string out from the bottom, then cut the strand into slices and enjoy.

2 quarts / 950 ml unsweetened pure grape juice
50 whole, large walnut halves
½ cup / 68 g unbleached all-purpose flour

In a medium saucepan, simmer the grape juice over very low heat, uncovered, for about 1½ hours, until the juice has reduced to about 3 cups / 700 ml. It's a good idea to check the juice after an hour to make sure it doesn't reduce too much. Let the juice stand in the saucepan overnight, covered.

In a 12-inch / 30 cm skillet, heat the walnut halves over very low heat until they are slightly toasted; alternatively, bake them at 350ºF / 175ºC for 6 to 8 minutes. Be careful not to let them brown. Set aside.

While the nuts are cooling, prepare the setup. Lay a dowel or clean broom handle across two chair seats of equal height and place newspaper underneath the dowel to catch any drips. Measure out two 3-foot / 91 cm lengths of ¹⁄₁₆-inch / 2 mm–thick twine. Thread a sturdy needle with one of the lengths, pulling the ends of the twine together at the bottom to tie into a knot.

Carefully thread a walnut half onto the twine, flat side up. The nuts are less likely to break if you find a spot slightly off center, rather than along the central ridge. It's not a problem if a little bit of the nut breaks off, but if it shatters, select another walnut half. Push the first strung walnut to a point 1½ inches / 4 cm above the knotted bottom. Keep stringing the nuts until you have threaded twenty-five of them onto the twine, each one flush against the next. Cut the needle from the twine at the top and knot the ends. Repeat with the second length of twine and the remaining twenty-five walnut halves. Set aside.

Place the flour in a medium bowl. Heat the grape juice to just below boiling and gradually whisk it into the flour, whisking vigorously so that lumps don't form. (If they do, simply put the juice through a fine-mesh sieve.) Return the juice to the saucepan and bring to a boil. Reduce the heat to low and cook for a few minutes, stirring, until the mixture thickens and no longer tastes of flour. CONTINUED ▶

Reduce the heat to its lowest setting. Take one strand of nuts and dip it repeatedly in the grape juice, using a spoon to pour juice over the top of the nuts so that they are completely coated. Carry the strand over to the chairs and loop it over the dowel. The excess juice will drip onto the newspaper. Repeat the procedure with the second strand, then remove the pan from the heat.

Allow the nuts to dry for 20 minutes. Then gently reheat the juice and dip each strand in it again to create a second layer of coating. If the juice gets too thick, whisk in a little grape juice, apple juice, or water to bring it to a workable consistency. Let the strands dry on the dowel a second time for 20 minutes, then repeat the process two more times, so that the nuts have four layers of coating.

Let the strands dry for about 4 days, or until they are no longer tacky to the touch, then remove them from the dowel. Wrap the strands in a clean kitchen towel and store at room temperature. Churchkhela keeps for a long time but is best when consumed within 3 to 4 months.

CHURCHKHELA WITH FRESH GRAPE JUICE

We call for bottled grape juice, but if you're up for a bit of labor, the finished confection will taste even better if you begin with fresh grapes. To do so, stem 5 pounds / 2.2 kg of red grapes and put them through a food mill. This task can be arduous if the skins are thick; it helps to crush the grapes first with a mallet. After the first round of pressing, pass the pulp through the food mill a couple more times to release as much juice as possible. Transfer the juice to a medium saucepan and simmer over very low heat, uncovered, for about 3 hours, until the juice has reduced by a little less than half to a fairly thick consistency. Then proceed as directed in the recipe.

SERVING SUGGESTIONS ENJOY AS A SNACK / CHOP INTO SALADS / ADD TO YOUR CHEESE PLATTER

Pickled Green Strawberries

Before they ripen into ruby-red fruits, strawberries take on a gorgeous pale jade coloration. At this stage, they are crisp and tart, but they lack the sweetness we adore. Brining them in vinegar, salt, and sugar delivers a pickle of unexpected charm. The texture, like that of a cucumber or under-ripe melon, offers a subtle crunch that gives way to a burst of acidity. Adding herbs to the pickling solution enhances the vegetal note.

Finding green strawberries can be a challenge, since juicy red summer strawberries are so beloved. If you can't grow your own, try befriending a local farmer or market purveyor and ask them to save some for you. Request light green, almost white berries that have no patches of red.

2 cups / 454 g green, unripe strawberries

A few dill, tarragon, or bronze fennel sprigs (optional, but recommended)

1½ cups / 360 ml raw, unfiltered apple cider vinegar

¾ cup / 175 ml water

3½ tablespoons / 45 g granulated sugar

3 tablespoons / 27 g kosher salt

Gently rinse the strawberries; leave the hulls intact. Place the berries in a 1-quart / 1 L jar or other nonreactive container. Drop in the herbs, if desired.

In a small saucepan over medium heat, warm the vinegar, water, sugar, and salt just until the sugar is completely dissolved. Cool the brine to room temperature, then pour it over the strawberries. Place a piece of plastic wrap or parchment directly on the surface to keep the fruit submerged. Close the jar tightly and leave at room temperature for 3 days, then refrigerate for 1 week before using. The strawberries will keep in the refrigerator for at least 3 months.

SERVING SUGGESTIONS SERVE ALONGSIDE FATTY MEATS OR PÂTÉ / ADD TO A CHEESE BOARD / DICE INTO CEVICHE / PURÉE INTO A FRUITY GAZPACHO / BLEND INTO A SMOOTHIE

Pickled Cherry and Rose Petal Jam

Cherry jam captures summer's brightness and warmth, and there's no denying that it's delicious in its traditional form. But our recipe brings the jam to another level by introducing two wildly different elements. First, we pickle the cherries instead of using fresh ones as the base for the jam. Then we add rose petals for a whiff of the floral that transports us into the summer garden.

It's crucial to use the right petals for this jam. They must be from aromatic roses, not scent-free hybrids and, of course, they must not have been sprayed with pesticide. If you can't find fresh petals, you can order dried ones online, though the rose flavor won't be quite as exquisite.

As a bonus, instead of discarding the liquid used to simmer the petals, stir in some lemon juice and honey to make a refreshing drink that can be enjoyed either hot or cold.

PICKLED CHERRIES

1 pound / 454 g sweet cherries, stemmed

¾ cup / 175 ml raw, unfiltered apple cider vinegar

¼ cup / 60 ml red wine vinegar

½ cup / 100 g sugar

2 teaspoons kosher salt

⅓ cup / 77 ml unsweetened cherry juice

JAM

1⅓ cups / 275 g sugar

Zest and juice of 1 lemon

4 ounces / 115 g fresh rose petals, removed from the stems, or 2 ounces / 56 g dried rose petals

⅓ cup / 80 ml reserved cherry pickling liquid

2 to 3 teaspoons / 10 to 15 ml rosewater

½ teaspoon citric acid

MAKE THE PICKLED CHERRIES: Put the cherries in a 2-quart / 2 L jar. Pour the apple cider vinegar and red wine vinegar over the cherries and leave them to sit overnight at room temperature. The next day, use a sieve to strain the vinegar into a medium saucepan. Return the cherries to the jar and close it with a lid.

Add the sugar, salt, and cherry juice to the vinegar in the pan and bring to a boil. Reduce the heat and simmer, uncovered, for 15 minutes. Cover the pan and cool the mixture to room temperature, then pour it over the cherries and close the lid. Leave the cherries to sit at room temperature for 3 days.

After 3 days, once again strain the liquid into a saucepan, return it to a boil, and simmer for 15 minutes. Cover the pan and cool to room temperature. Pour the liquid over the cherries and close the lid. Place the jar in a cool, dark place and let the cherries sit for at least 2 weeks before using.

MAKE THE JAM: Drain the cherries in a sieve, reserving the pickling liquid, then pit them and place in a wide, heavy pan. Stir in the sugar and lemon zest. Cover the pot and leave the cherries to macerate overnight at room temperature.

The next day, prepare the rose petals by cutting off the white base with a pair of scissors to avoid any bitterness. In a separate saucepan, combine the rose petals with the lemon juice and enough water to cover. Simmer for 15 minutes, then drain the petals thoroughly, pressing down on them lightly with a kitchen towel to make sure that all the liquid has been expelled and the petals are as dry as possible.

Place a small plate in the freezer for testing the jam. Add ⅓ cup/80 ml of the reserved pickling liquid to the cherries, stirring well. Slowly bring the cherry mixture to a boil over low heat. Simmer for about 15 minutes, stirring frequently, until the cherries just begin to buckle and soften. Add the rose petals and simmer for another 20 to 30 minutes, stirring frequently, until both the cherries and the rose petals are tender. At this point the bubbles should be very small.

Test the jam for a set by dropping a spoonful onto the chilled plate. Put it in the refrigerator for a few minutes, then run your finger through the mixture; if it wrinkles, it's done. Add the rosewater and citric acid to the cherries in the pan and stir well. Ladle the hot jam into sterilized jars and place a small piece of wax paper or parchment directly on the surface. Seal the jars and refrigerate. The jam will last for 6 months. For longer storage, see Notes on Canning (page 99).

SERVING SUGGESTIONS   DOLLOP ONTO ICE CREAM OR CUSTARD / SLATHER ON TOAST WITH MELTED CHEESE / USE IN THUMBPRINT COOKIES

Pear and Apple Spread

This spread is a riff on two popular fruit preparations from neighboring regions of Germany and Belgium. At harvest time, cooks on both sides of the border prepare a conserve by cooking down apples and pears into a thick, molasses-like syrup that they locally call "kraut" (not to be confused with the word used elsewhere for cabbage!). Germans use more apples in their Rheinisches Apfelkraut, *Belgians more pears in their* sirop de Liège.

Our version is a little more Belgian, favoring pears over apples, with a few added dates. Rather than filtering the purée to get a clear juice, we simply cook it down into a soft spread to retain the fruits' nutrients and concentrate their flavors. We favor using a slow cooker so we don't have to stand over the stove stirring for hours to ensure that the fruit doesn't burn. The result is a naturally sweet spread that's delectable enough to eat right out of the jar.

6 pounds / 2.72 kg pears, such as Bartlett, quartered (do not peel or core)

2 pounds / 900 g tart apples, such as Granny Smith, quartered (do not peel or core)

5 large Medjool dates, pitted and coarsely chopped

Place all the ingredients in a large (6-quart / 6 L) slow cooker and cook, covered, on the "low" setting until the fruit has broken down, about 4 hours, stirring once or twice to distribute the softening fruit. If you don't have a slow cooker, cook the pears, apples, and dates in a large, heavy pot on a stovetop burner's lowest possible heat, stirring occasionally, until the fruit has broken down, about 1 hour.

Pass the fruit through a food mill to yield a thick purée. You should have about 3 quarts / 3 L.

Return the purée to the slow cooker and continue to cook on low, uncovered, until it has thickened nicely and has reduced by half, stirring occasionally. This process will take 6 to 8 hours. If desired, continue cooking the purée down until it is as thick as a stiff fruit butter or jam. If using a stovetop, the process will take up to 2 hours, and you'll need to stir frequently to make sure the fruit doesn't burn.

Pour the spread into sterilized pint jars and seal. The spread will keep in the refrigerator for 2 to 3 months. For longer storage, see Notes on Canning (page 99).

SERVING SUGGESTIONS LAYER WITH CREPES / SERVE WITH POTATO PANCAKES IN PLACE OF APPLESAUCE / ADD A SPOONFUL TO HEARTY BEEF STEWS LIKE SAUERBRATEN OR CARBONNADE / USE IN JAMMY OAT BARS (PAGE 65)

Jammy Oat Bars

Toasted oats and spelt flour give these bar cookies a wonderfully nutty taste, while jam provides a sweet lift. The bars resemble shortbread in their butteriness, and old-fashioned crumbles in their texture—a winning combination. They're also a good opportunity for experimenting with different fillings to create your favorite flavor profiles. For a more formal presentation, keep the shortbread whole and serve it on a cake platter for dessert. Cut into bars at the table.

1 cup/84 g old-fashioned rolled oats
1 cup/125 g unbleached all-purpose flour
½ cup/60 g spelt flour
⅔ cup/80 g confectioners' sugar
1 tablespoon firmly packed dark brown sugar
¼ cup/28 g cornstarch
¾ teaspoon kosher salt
1 teaspoon ground cardamom
Zest of 1 lemon
14 tablespoons/199 g cold unsalted butter, cut into ⅛-inch/3 mm slices
Generous 1 cup/350 g Pear and Apple Spread (page 62), Pickled Cherry and Rose Petal Jam (page 58), or other favorite jam

Preheat the oven to 350°F/175°C. Lightly brush an 8 by 8-inch/20 by 20 cm baking pan with a neutral vegetable oil and line it with parchment paper, using enough so that the paper hangs over two edges; this will enable you to lift the shortbread from the pan.

Spread the oats on a parchment-lined baking sheet and toast them in the oven for 10 to 12 minutes, stirring once halfway through, until they are golden brown and fragrant. Remove them from the oven but leave the oven on.

Transfer ½ cup/42 g of the cooled oats to the bowl of a stand mixer fitted with the paddle attachment. Put the remaining ½ cup/42 g of oats in a blender or food processor and whir them into a fine powder. Add the powdered oats to the mixing bowl along with the all-purpose flour, spelt flour, confectioners' sugar, brown sugar, cornstarch, salt, cardamom, and lemon zest. Mix on low speed just until combined. Add the butter, one piece at a time, and mix on low for about 8 minutes, until the mixture begins to hold together. It will still be crumbly.

Pour three-quarters of the crumb mixture into the prepared pan. With your fingers, press it evenly over the bottom of the pan to form a solid layer. Prick this base all over with the tines of a fork. Bake the shortbread for 15 to 20 minutes, until the edges turn pale brown.

Remove the pan from the oven and spread the jam over the shortbread, leaving a ¼-inch/6 mm border around the edges. Crumble the remaining dough over the jam in random fashion, leaving areas of jam exposed, and press down on it gently. Bake the shortbread for 30 to 40 minutes, until golden brown.

Cool the shortbread in the pan for 15 minutes, then use the overhanging parchment to lift it from the pan onto a wire rack. Cool the shortbread completely before cutting it into bars. The cookies taste even better the second day. Stored in an airtight container at room temperature, they will keep for up to a week.

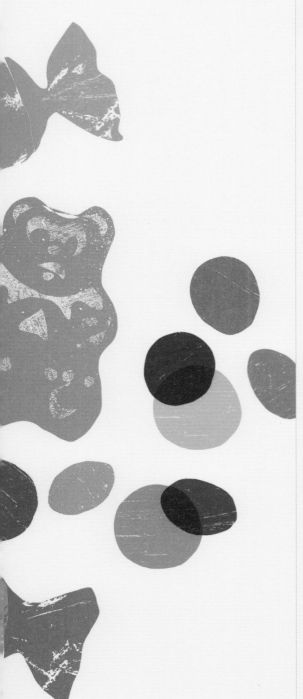

SUGAR RUSH

Preserved fruit—eaten for millennia as a source of nourishment or as a sweet treat—hit the American mainstream in the first half of the twentieth century, fueled by revolutionary new marketing techniques and innovations in food science combined with the particularly American embrace of convenience. Kool-Aid, Welch's grape jelly, and Del Monte fruit cocktail are a few of the now-classic items that debuted with a flourish.

These time-saving products gave people what they wanted, namely sweet, fruity flavors, without the laborious work of turning fresh fruit into syrups, jellies, or concentrates at home, as their forebears had done.

What we now know as Del Monte canned fruit cocktail evolved from such nineteenth-century fruit salads as ambrosia—a sweet mix of grated coconut, sliced oranges, and sugar—and other combinations of diced or sliced pieces of fruit. California canneries developed the idea for canned fruit cocktail to cut down on waste, packaging the bits of peaches, pears, and pineapples that couldn't be used for whole canned fruits. Preserved in syrup, the sweet, fruity concoction caught on after its introduction in the 1930s, and while not as popular today as it once was, fruit cocktail is still a supermarket staple.

Fruit cocktail also served as something of a blueprint for brands to develop preserved fruits into highly marketable, colorfully packaged products. Jams, jellies, syrups, candies, powders, sugared fruits, and dried fruits and fruit leathers became cogs in a hyper-industrializing America, fueling growth that accelerated after World War II and helping to spawn what is today a trillion-dollar market for consumer-packaged goods. To kids, however, the grapes in their peanut butter and jelly sandwiches and the powdered strawberry stirred into their milk simply tasted tantalizingly good, offering a hit of sweetness in their daily diet.

The sweet, fruity cereals and sugar-packed juices that the post–World War II generations were raised on seemed like blissful indulgences. We now know that added sugars and artificially sweetened foods can wreak havoc on human health, but for a good half century a celebratory vibe surrounded these products and brands, which became ingrained in the American consciousness. Companies and their advertising agencies took the fruit cocktail concept to the next level, amping up the color saturation and slogans on packaging and supercharging the flavors to meet the American appetite for sweetness.

Ironically, most of the hyped-up products of this modern era trace their lineage back to the earliest forms of fruit preservation. The ancient art of dehydrating fruit in the sun produces fruit leather, which became the inspiration for several twentieth-century dried fruit treats, the most famous of which, Fruit Roll-Ups, caught on with 1980s kids who loved peeling the artificially flavored fruit-like product and wrapping it around their fingers before consuming it. Dannon's fruit-enhanced yogurts debuted in the late 1940s in the Bronx, when the company's French-American owner— who had been producing plain, unsweetened yogurt—added a strawberry compote to be

mixed into the yogurt to appeal to the American sweets-loving palate, thereby launching a juggernaut of creamy fruit-on-the-bottom yogurts that are still immensely popular today.

Fruit syrups likewise inspired Americanized reinventions, and brands such as Smucker's and Aunt Jemima, as well as restaurant chains like International House of Pancakes, joined those mentioned above in promoting the fruits, so to speak, of our ancestors' labors. Only now their products had very little nutritional value and more often than not contained artificial flavors.

Commercial candies also took inspiration from fruit, and not only in the United States, the birthplace of the Jolly Rancher. Chewy fruit-flavored squares of Starburst started out as Opal Fruits in England, where button-shaped Skittles also first appeared. They gained widespread popularity only after getting an American makeover and a catchphrase, "Taste the Rainbow." Japan's beloved Kasugai lychee and peach gummies, German Haribo gummies, and Swedish Kolsvart elderberry gummies continue an ancient tradition of finding ways to make the fleeting flavors of summer endure, while guaranteeing a sugar rush to boot.

Whenever you want superlative flavor in fruits—

ask for DEL MONTE—the brand preferred by more women than any other line of canned fruits and vegetables in the world! So many delicious varieties, too!

Del Monte

Del Monte
BRAND QUALITY
CANNED FRUITS

Pineapple • Apricots
Peaches • Fruit Cocktail
Fruits for Salad • Pears

Plums • Cherries
Grapefruit • Prunes
Figs • and others

More good foods
from the brand that puts
FLAVOR FIRST

Very Berry Maple Syrup

Some people swear by maple syrup on their pancakes and waffles. Others prefer berries at the breakfast table, either served fresh as a fruit topping or as a clear syrup. Here, we unite the two schools of taste by mixing berries with maple syrup. The result is a fruity, full-bodied syrup with a sweet and sour flavor, thanks to the addition of honey and whey plus a few days of fermentation. If you use raspberries or blackberries, the syrup will contain seeds, which we happen to like; if you prefer a clear syrup, you can always strain them out before refrigerating.

1 pound /454 g berries, such as raspberries, blackberries, strawberries, or blueberries, or a combination

¼ cup /60 ml fresh whey, strained from plain, full-fat yogurt

2 tablespoons /42 g raw, unpasteurized honey

1¼ teaspoons kosher salt

¾ cup /240 g pure maple syrup, preferably dark Grade B

In a blender, briefly pulse the berries, whey, honey, and salt just until the berries have broken up. Pour the mixture into a 1-quart / 1 L jar and close the lid tightly. Leave on the counter at room temperature (68° to 72°F/ 20° to 22°C) to ferment for 3 days.

After 3 days, stir in the maple syrup. Leave the mixture on the counter for 1 more day. The syrup can be refrigerated as is, or you can strain it first to remove any seeds. The syrup will keep for up to 2 months.

SERVING SUGGESTIONS USE ON PANCAKES, WAFFLES, AND CREPES / STIR INTO SMOOTHIES / SPOON OVER YOGURT OR FROZEN CUSTARD

Candied Quince

Of all candied fruits, quince undergoes the most dramatic transformation: when subjected to heat, it turns from pale yellow to stunning vermilion. And yet, despite its beauty, quince remains at the margins of popularity, and not only because it looks like a giant prehistoric pear. In its raw state, the fruit is practically inedible, so hard and astringent that one bite causes an intense pucker. Cooking allows the beauty of the quince to bloom, releasing its floral aroma and mellow sweetness.

Our recipe calls for soaking the raw fruit overnight in a pickling lime solution to ensure that the finished candy has a nice chew. For a lovely note of pine and pepper, we add cardamom to the sugar syrup.

---

3 tablespoons / 21 g calcium hydroxide powder (pickling lime)

2 quarts / 2 L water

1 pound / 454 g quince, peeled, quartered, and cut into wedges

5 cups plus 2 tablespoons / 1,020 g sugar

9 green cardamom pods, plus more if desired

9 tablespoons / 135 ml freshly squeezed lemon juice

Bay leaf (optional)

In a large bowl, whisk the pickling lime with 4 cups / 1 L of the water until the lime dissolves. Add the quince wedges and leave them to soak overnight, making sure they are completely submerged. The next morning, drain and rinse the quince wedges several times, then place them on a kitchen towel to drain.

In a heavy pot over medium heat, gently warm the remaining 4 cups / 1 L of water with the sugar and cardamom pods, without stirring, until the sugar dissolves. Increase the heat to high and boil the syrup for 18 to 20 minutes, until it has thickened slightly. Resist the urge to stir the syrup, as this can cause it to crystallize. If any crystals form on the side of the pot, use a pastry brush dipped in water to gently wipe them away.

While the syrup is cooking, bring a large saucepan of water to a boil. Add the quince wedges, return the water to boiling, and blanch them for 2 to 3 minutes, depending on their size. Drain, refresh them with cold water, and drain again.

Add the drained quinces to the prepared syrup and simmer for 1½ to 2 hours, or until the wedges turn slightly translucent, skimming any foam that rises to the surface as they cook. Do not stir the syrup; if any sugar begins to crystallize on the sides of the pan, again wipe it off with a wet pastry brush.

After an hour of cooking, add the lemon juice, and continue to cook the syrup until it has thickened to the consistency of honey and reaches 225° to 228°F / 107° to 109°C on a candy thermometer. (If the syrup has thickened too much, add a little water to the pot and let it simmer briefly until the syrup has thinned to the right consistency.)

Leave the quinces to cool, then transfer them along with the syrup into a 1-quart / 1 L jar. If desired, add a few fresh cardamom pods or a bay leaf for additional flavor. The quinces will keep indefinitely in the refrigerator.

SERVING SUGGESTIONS ENJOY AS A SWEET SNACK / MAKE INTO A TARTE TATIN / ROLL IN FINELY CHOPPED PISTACHIOS AND SERVE AS PART OF A PLATE OF SWEETS / SERVE WITH POT DE CRÈME, ICE CREAM, OR YOGURT

Spicy Citrus Peel Paste

Citrus fruits must be peeled to get at the juicy flesh hiding within. Still, it's a shame to discard the rinds, since they contain highly flavorful essential oils that can be put to good use in the kitchen. So, begin by grinding the peel with aromatic spices, then adding lime juice and vinegar for brightness. A goodly amount of chile powder contributes an exhilarating zing, while a little vegetable oil turns the mixture into a spreadable paste.

You can use this paste as you would any spice rub or marinade. Or take inspiration from the fermented Japanese citrus paste known as yuzu kosho, *and use citrus peel paste as a finishing condiment in soups and braises.*

1½ pounds / 700 g fresh citrus

1 teaspoon fenugreek seed, toasted

1 teaspoon mustard seed, toasted

1 teaspoon coriander seed, toasted

3 tablespoons plus 1 teaspoon / 30 g kosher salt

2 tablespoons plus 1 teaspoon / 15 g red chile powder (or less, to taste), such as Kashmiri, ancho, or Aleppo

2¾ teaspoons granulated sugar

4 teaspoons freshly squeezed lime juice

2 teaspoons champagne vinegar

¼ cup / 60 ml grapeseed oil

With a flat-head peeler, peel the rind from the fruit, being careful to avoid the bitter white pith. You should have about 4 ounces / 125 g. Chop the rind coarsely. Reserve the flesh for another use.

In a blender, pulse the fenugreek, mustard, and coriander seeds into a coarse powder. Add the citrus peel, salt, chile powder, sugar, lime juice, and vinegar. Purée into a smooth paste. Pour in the oil and purée on high speed for 15 seconds. Transfer the mixture to a small jar. The paste will keep for at least 1 month in the refrigerator.

SERVING SUGGESTIONS USE AS A SPICE RUB FOR FISH OR MEAT / SWIRL INTO YOGURT FOR A COOLING CONDIMENT / STIR INTO RICE

Tutti Frutti

Tutti frutti, a nearly everlasting combination of brandy-soaked fruits, became the height of culinary fashion in the 1880s. Its Italian name (which means "all fruits") lent cachet to a very basic method of preserving seasonal fruits in brandy. It proved so popular that in 1888, the first vending machine in America sold Tutti Frutti chewing gum. But the advent of Prohibition, with its interdiction of alcohol, killed the beloved fruit mixture. Fortunately, the flavor itself didn't disappear, just the brandy. In the 1920s "tutti frutti" came to refer to finely chopped dried or candied fruit blends that were added to ice cream or used as a sandwich filling. Today, it's still possible to buy a popular brand of rum ice cream dotted with candied fruits and pecans.

The original tutti frutti is due for a comeback. Just begin with a base of brandy and sugar, then add an early summer fruit. As each new fruit ripens, stir it into the crock along with its weight in sugar (once the tutti frutti is established, you can cut back slightly on the additional sugar). Feel free to substitute or add other fruits, like grapes or plums. Stored in a cool, dark place, the tutti frutti will improve with age, and you can keep your mixture going for years, dipping in whenever fancy strikes. If, like us, you keep ice cream tucked away in the freezer, a ladle of tutti frutti spooned over ice cream will dazzle any unexpected guests.

BASE

1½ cups / 350 ml brandy

1 cup / 200 g granulated sugar

FRUIT

8 ounces / 227 g strawberries, hulled and halved (or quartered, if large)

5½ to 6 cups / 1 to 1.1 kg granulated sugar or sucanat

2 (6-inch / 15 cm) spirals of orange peel

8 ounces / 225 g peaches, pitted and cut into ½-inch / 1.25 cm chunks

8 ounces / 225 g sweet cherries, stemmed, pitted, and halved

8 ounces / 225 g pineapple, peeled, cored, and cut into ½-inch / 1.25 cm chunks

8 ounces / 225 g pears, peeled, cored, and cut into ½-inch / 1.25 cm chunks

MAKE THE BASE: Sterilize a 2-quart / 2 L ceramic crock or wide-mouth glass jar. Pour the brandy into the container and stir in the sugar until dissolved.

ADD THE FRUIT: Stir in the strawberries and 1¼ cups / 225 g of the sugar. Then stir in the orange peel. Press a piece of parchment paper onto the surface and cover the crock or jar tightly. (If the lid of the crock isn't tight-fitting, cover the parchment with a piece of plastic wrap and then place the lid on top.) Set aside in a cool, dark place for 3 days.

Add the peaches to the crock, along with another 1¼ cups / 225 g of sugar, stirring well to dissolve the sugar. You can either add the rest of the fruit and sugar now, or add the fruit sequentially as it comes into season, along with its weight in sugar. Always stir well after each addition.

The tutti frutti will be ready after a few weeks, but the flavors continue to develop the longer it sits. You can replenish it by adding new fruit and sugar to replace whatever you've removed, or renew it with a spoonful or two of apricot jam.

SERVING SUGGESTIONS STIR INTO YOGURT / ADD THE SOAKED FRUIT TO PUDDINGS AND PIES / USE THE SYRUP IN CAKE BATTER AND THE DRAINED FRUIT BETWEEN BAKED CAKE LAYERS

Tutti Frutti Fruitcake

Fruitcake gets a bad rap. So, instead of the commercial brands studded with neon glacé fruit, we propose a version that's dark and rich like a boozy energy bar. It's high in protein from plenty of nuts and is filled with natural dried fruits. The whole wheat and buckwheat flours amplify its wholesomeness.

Disdainers of fruitcake may be surprised to learn that, in the past, fruitcakes were considered prestigious. Because the many pieces of diced fruits and nuts symbolized fertility, fruitcakes were once served at weddings. A heavy fruitcake called a groom's cake was popular in seventeenth-century England, where it was offered alongside the bride's cake. The fruitcake was cut up into small squares for wedding favors; an unmarried woman who placed a piece of cake under her pillow was prophesied to dream of the man she would marry.

Eventually fruitcake became a celebratory staple of the Christmas holidays. Although you can eat the cake as soon as it has cooled, both the flavor and texture improve with aging, especially when the cake is moistened with alcohol. Spirits were originally added to help preserve the cake for months—even years—leading to numerous jokes and legends about fruitcake's longevity. We use rum, but you can substitute brandy, whiskey, sherry, bourbon, or even Guinness to achieve the taste you prefer.

This fruitcake can be baked a good three months before you plan to serve it. If you're not up to dicing so much fruit, feel free to substitute an equal amount of packaged baker's dried fruit medley, available online.

1 firmly packed cup / 160 g tart dried cherries
1 firmly packed cup / 60 g diced dried apples
¾ cup / 110 g golden raisins
½ cup / 100 g diced dried pears
½ cup / 85 g diced dried apricots
½ cup / 75 g diced dried peaches
½ cup / 75 g diced dried figs
¼ cup / 35 g diced candied ginger
¼ cup / 75 g diced dried dates
½ cup / 64 g shelled raw, unsalted pistachios, toasted and coarsely chopped
½ cup / 64 g pine nuts, toasted
½ cup / 50 g pecans, toasted and coarsely chopped
Zest of 1 lemon
Zest of 1 orange
1¼ cups / 300 ml dark rum
½ cup / 120 ml syrup from Tutti Frutti jar (page 80) or apple cider
¼ cup / 60 ml raw, unfiltered apple cider vinegar

1 cup / 120 g whole wheat flour
½ cup plus 2 tablespoons / 100 g buckwheat flour
1¾ teaspoons baking soda
1 teaspoon kosher salt
1 teaspoon ground cinnamon
1 teaspoon ground ginger
1 teaspoon ground cardamom
¾ teaspoon ground nutmeg
½ teaspoon baking powder
¼ teaspoon ground cloves
½ cup / 113 g unsalted butter, at room temperature
¼ cup / 55 g dark muscovado sugar
¼ cup / 85 g raw, unpasteurized honey (omit if using Tutti Frutti syrup)
1 large egg
Rum, for aging the cake

Combine the dried cherries, dried apples, raisins, dried pears, dried apricots, dried peaches, dried figs, candied ginger, dried dates, pistachios, pine nuts, pecans, lemon zest, and orange zest in a large bowl.

In a small saucepan over medium heat, combine the rum, tutti frutti syrup, and vinegar and bring to a boil. Remove the pan from the heat and pour the liquid over the fruits and nuts. Cover the bowl and leave the mixture to steep at room temperature overnight.

The next day, preheat the oven to 350°F/175°C. Butter a 10-inch/25 cm loaf or springform pan and line it with parchment paper.

In a large bowl, combine the whole wheat flour, buckwheat flour, baking soda, salt, cinnamon, ginger, cardamom, nutmeg, baking powder, and cloves and mix well.

In the bowl of a stand mixer fitted with the whisk attachment, combine the butter, muscovado sugar, and honey. Beat the mixture on high until light, periodically scraping down the sides. Gradually beat in the egg until it is well incorporated—don't worry if the mixture looks curdled. On low speed, add the dry ingredients in three batches, mixing well after each addition. The mixture will look dry. Switch to the paddle attachment; on low speed, add the fruits and nuts, and any liquid that hasn't been absorbed, mixing only enough to thoroughly combine.

Scrape the batter into the loaf pan, smoothing the top. Tent the top loosely with a piece of aluminum foil to keep the cake from browning too fast. Bake for 75 to 90 minutes, until a cake tester comes out clean. Turn off the heat and leave the cake to cool in the oven for 1 hour.

Transfer the loaf to a rack to let the cake cool completely, which will take several hours. Once the cake is cool, carefully remove it from the pan and return it to the cooling rack. Leave the cake to sit overnight, uncovered, to dry out a bit.

Moisten a large piece of cheesecloth with rum until it is slightly damp, not soaking. Wrap the cake tightly in the cheesecloth, then cover it with waxed paper and aluminum foil. Place the cake in a large zip-top bag. Store it in a cool, dark place for at least 4 weeks, unwrapping the cheesecloth and renewing the rum once a week. The cake will keep for at least 3 months.

Fruit Leather and Fruit Paste

Summer fruits can be tricky. We wait impatiently for them to ripen, and suddenly, there they are, in all their bounty, and we race to preserve them at their peak, boiling them into jams or chutneys and laboriously canning them. Here we offer a simpler alternative with two relaxed recipes that transform summer fruits into long-lasting delicacies by concentrating their natural sweetness. No sugar or stovetop cooking needed! You can use plums, peaches, cherries, and berries to make fruit leathers and fruit pastes.

For both Fruit Leather and Fruit Paste (page 88), the amount of fruit to start with is extremely flexible. Just be sure to spread the purée very thinly before dehydrating it. You can adapt the recipes to your own taste by combining a variety of fruits or by mixing the fruit with a little lemon juice, maple syrup, or spices such as cinnamon, cardamom, or freshly grated ginger.

FRUIT LEATHER

1 pound / 454 g ripe summer fruit
Spices or other seasonings (optional)

Set a dehydrator to 120°F / 50°C or preheat the oven to 140°F / 60°C. Line a rimmed baking sheet or dehydrator rack with a nonstick silicone mat or parchment paper.

Remove any bruised parts from the fruit and prepare each type as needed, removing the pits from stone fruits, hulling strawberries, and so on. Place the fruit in a blender, along with any desired seasonings, and purée until it is as smooth as possible. Strain out any chunks.

Pour the fruit onto the prepared baking sheet and spread it evenly into a 9 by 12-inch / 23 by 30 cm rectangle that is approximately ⅛ inch / 3 mm thick. Make the edges a bit thicker than the center since they will cook more quickly. Be careful not to spread the purée too thinly or it will be hard to peel off the sheet.

Bake or dehydrate until the mixture is dry to the touch. The timing will depend on the method you're using and on how juicy the fruit is. Oven-dried leather will take approximately 8 hours; in a dehydrator, the leather will be ready in about 24 hours. It's a good idea to check the purée periodically beginning after 4 hours to make sure it doesn't become too hard. The finished leather should be dry but supple.

Remove the leather from the oven or dehydrator and leave it to cool completely. Then, starting at one end, gently peel the leather off the silicone or parchment. It can be stored as a single sheet or cut into 3 by 6-inch / 7.5 by 15 cm strips for individual servings. Place each piece of leather on a piece of parchment paper and roll it up like a scroll. Tie the roll with twine and store at room temperature in an airtight container for up to 3 months.

SERVING SUGGESTIONS WRAP WITH PARCHMENT AND TWINE FOR A LOVELY HOSTESS GIFT / EAT AS A NATURALLY SWEET SNACK / CUT INTO THIN STRIPS AND SIMMER IN SOUPS AND STEWS CONTINUED ▶

FRUIT LEATHER AND FRUIT PASTE CONTINUED

FRUIT PASTE

5 pounds / 2.2 kg ripe fruit, hulled, peeled,
     pitted, or cored as necessary
Spices or other seasonings (optional)

In a blender, purée the fruit and optional
seasonings (in batches, if necessary) until completely smooth. Pour the purée into one or two
9 by 13-inch / 23 by 33 cm glass baking dishes,
depending on how much juice your fruit has
produced, making sure that the layers are no
more than about 1½ inches / 4 cm deep.

Dehydrate the purée at 125ºF / 52ºC. If you
don't have a dehydrator, cover and bake it at
170ºF / 77ºC. Stir every 3 to 4 hours to break up
any skin that forms on the surface. The paste is
ready when it has reached the consistency of
applesauce.

Transfer the paste to a blender and purée once
again until very smooth. Spoon it into a jar and
press a piece of plastic wrap or parchment
paper onto the surface of the paste. Close and
refrigerate for up to 1 year.

SERVING SUGGESTIONS SPREAD ON
TOAST / USE BETWEEN CAKE LAYERS / ADD
TO CHAMPAGNE COCKTAILS / WHISK INTO
MAPLE SYRUP FOR A FRUITY HIT

Pomegranate Molasses

Although we call this tart-sweet condiment "molasses," it contains no sweetener. This "molasses" is a concentrate made by boiling down the juice of ripe pomegranates until thick and syrupy. As the juice slowly reduces, it oxidizes, turning the bright red of fresh pomegranates into a mahogany syrup similar in color and consistency to molasses. It can be used like balsamic vinegar: drizzled over roasted vegetables for a bright finish or added to salad dressings. It also adds a wonderfully fruity note to soups and stews, such as the Persian chicken and walnut dish fesanjan.

Prying the arils from the pomegranates' thick membrane is admittedly a time-consuming project. We consider this type of hands-on work worthwhile—such labor adds a certain element of satisfaction to the finished syrup—but we also recognize time constraints. So we offer two graceful shortcuts, one using arils that have already been separated from the membrane, the other simply using bottled pomegranate juice.

6½ pounds / 3 kg fresh pomegranates,
or 10 cups / 1.8 kg pomegranate arils,
or 5½ cups / 1.3 L unsweetened
pomegranate juice

If using fresh pomegranates, cut a ¼-inch / 6 mm slice off the stem end (bottom) of the pomegranate, being careful not to expose any of the bright red fruit. Place the pomegranate on the cutting board cut-side down. Use a small paring knife to carve a shallow circle all the way around the blossom end to expose the white pith, again being careful not to reveal any of the fruit.

Fill a large bowl with about 1 inch / 2.5 cm of water. Make six shallow vertical slits around the pomegranate, cutting only through the thick red skin from the blossom end to the stem end. Working over the bowl, gently pry the pomegranate open with your fingers, pulling the skin away. You will begin to see the bright red arils, which are covered by a membrane of white pith. After all the skin has been removed, carefully free the arils from the membrane.

Skim the discarded membranes from the water, then drain the arils. You should have about 10 cups / 1.8 kg. Use immediately or refrigerate in an airtight container for up to 4 days.

To make the pomegranate juice, set a cheesecloth-lined sieve over a nonreactive bowl. In small batches, gently pulse the arils in a blender or food processor for 5 to 10 seconds, just until the juice starts to separate from the seeds, scraping down the sides periodically (the inner seeds can be bitter, so try not to purée them into the juice). Pour the mash into the sieve. Squeeze out as much juice as you can by wringing the cheesecloth tightly. Repeat with the rest of the arils. You should end up with 5½ cups / 1.3 L of juice.

Pour the juice into a wide, shallow 12-inch / 30 cm sauté pan over low heat and let it simmer slowly, uncovered (at around 200°F / 95°C on a candy thermometer), periodically scraping the sides of the pan. Do not let the juice boil. Continue to cook until it is thick enough to coat the back of a spoon and your finger leaves a clean line when drawn through it; this can take up to 1½ hours from start to finish. The juice will have reduced to ¾ to 1 cup / 175 to 240 ml. Cool the juice, then pour it into a small jar. The pomegranate molasses will keep, covered, in the refrigerator for at least 6 months.

SERVING SUGGESTIONS USE TO GLAZE MEATS, SUCH AS LAMB, DUCK, OR CHICKEN LEGS / WHISK INTO SALAD DRESSINGS / STIR INTO ICED TEA, LEMONADE, OR YOUR FAVORITE COCKTAIL

Cranberry-Orange Shrub

The history of the infused vinegar drink known as shrub is, shall we say, muddled. The word shrub *doesn't in this case refer to a plant; instead, it derives from the Arabic* sharāb, *or beverage. Ancient Persians made a refreshing drink known as* sharbat, *which they prepared by mixing grated cucumber and mint into a syrup of vinegar and honey. By the time sharbat made its way to Western Europe in the sixteenth century, citrus juice had replaced vinegar, and the drink was called "sherbet." Within another century the British were adding copious amounts of brandy or other liquor to the drink and calling it "shrub."*

In the American colonies, where citrus fruits were hard to obtain, vinegar once again became the souring agent of choice. In the nineteenth century, shrubs experienced a heyday. Besides providing refreshment, they had the added benefit of preserving the fruit used to make them.

Shrubs are enjoying a revival these days, since their sweet-and-sour fruitiness adds pizzazz to mixed drinks and nonalcoholic punches. You'll find our cranberry-orange shrub equally refreshing as a cooling summer beverage or as a special libation at cold-weather feasts.

2 cups / 240 g cranberries

½ cup / 170 g orange blossom honey

2 tablespoons / 12 g peeled and grated fresh ginger

½ cup / 120 ml raw, unfiltered apple cider vinegar

½ cup / 120 ml red wine vinegar

¾ teaspoon orange blossom water (optional)

1 tablespoon dried orange blossoms

In a small saucepan, combine the cranberries, honey, and ginger. Simmer just until warm, about 5 minutes; the fruit shouldn't be very cooked. Transfer the mixture to a blender along with the cider vinegar, wine vinegar, and orange blossom water and purée until smooth. Stir in the orange blossoms, then transfer the mixture to a 1-quart / 1 L jar. Press a piece of parchment paper or plastic wrap directly against the surface of the purée, then cap the jar tightly. Leave to infuse at room temperature for 4 days. Strain the mixture through a fine sieve, pressing hard on the solids to extract all of the liquid. Discard the solids. Pour the shrub into an airtight container and refrigerate for up to 3 months.

SERVING SUGGESTIONS MAKE A SPARKLING NONALCOHOLIC DRINK BY MIXING 1 ½ OUNCES / 44 ML SHRUB WITH 4 OUNCES / 118 ML SPARKLING WATER / USE IN COCKTAIL MIXES / STIR INTO SAUCES AND VINAIGRETTES

Green Plum and Fig Leaf Elixir

Maesil cheong is a Korean green plum syrup used for a variety of purposes. Not only is it a sweetener and a beloved tea, it's used as a remedy for digestive issues and even the common cold—though too often the syrup is made these days with sugar instead of honey, thereby losing some of its healthful properties. Here, we nod to tradition by fermenting the plums in granulated honey, which is honey that has been crystallized with sugar and dried, before milling into granules. To add a bewitching herbal note, we layer the plums with fresh fig leaves.

Making the syrup takes considerable patience—you need to wait a good ninety days before it is ready. But once made, maesil cheong will last forever. When straining the syrup, don't just toss the honey-soaked plums. You can use them instead to make fruit scrap vinegar, or remove the pits and dry the plums for a snack. You can also simmer the plums with a splash of water and pass them through a food mill to make a fruity purée to stir into desserts.

1 pound / 454 g green plums, such as
　　greengage
6 fresh fig leaves or other fresh aromatics, such
　　as bronze fennel
1 pound / 454 g granulated honey crystals
3 tablespoons / 32 g bee pollen

Using a paring knife, score each plum three times horizontally about halfway through to the pit to allow the fruit's juices to release into the honey.

Place a fig leaf at the bottom of a 1-gallon / 4 L glass jar. Then begin alternating layers of the scored plums with the granulated honey and bee pollen, placing fig leaves on every other layer or so, reserving one to go on top. Once all the ingredients have been used, place a piece of plastic wrap directly on the surface, then add a stone or fermentation weight to keep the plums submerged. Cover the jar tightly with a lid.

Set the jar in a cool, dark spot for 7 days. Then remove the lid, weight, and plastic cover. Give the plums a stir; at this point most, if not all, of the honey granules should be moistened with plum juice. Re-cover the plums with plastic wrap, add the weight, seal the jar, and leave for 90 days, stirring once every couple of weeks.

Begin tasting the cheong after 90 days. Once you like the concentration of flavor, strain the syrup and refrigerate it. The elixir will keep indefinitely.

SERVING SUGGESTIONS STIR 2 TO 3 TABLE-SPOONS / 30 TO 45 ML INTO 1 CUP / 240 ML HOT WATER FOR A HEALING TEA / MIX INTO SPARKLING WATER / USE AS A SIMPLE SYRUP IN COCKTAILS / ADD TO MARINADES FOR A NUANCED SWEETNESS / THE STEEPED PLUMS CAN BE EATEN AS A SWEET TREAT

NOTES ON CANNING

Preserves can be processed in a water bath for longer-term storage. Use sturdy glass canning jars with two-piece lids—a flat lid with rubber edges and a metal ring. Before filling the jars, sterilize them by placing them on a rack in a canning pot or large stockpot. Cover the jars with hot water, place a lid on the pot, and bring to a boil. Boil for 10 minutes. Place the jar lids and other utensils you plan to use in a separate smaller pot and simmer for 10 minutes. The jars and lids can remain in the water until you're ready to use them, as long as they remain hot.

Use tongs to lift the jars from the pot and pour out the water. Set the jars upright on a kitchen towel on the counter. Working quickly, fill the jars to the top with your preserves, leaving ½ inch / 1.3 cm of headspace, as ingredients can expand during the canning process. With a paper towel, carefully wipe away any preserves that might have spilled onto the rim. If any air bubbles have formed, run a blunt knife around the edges of the jar to remove them. Immediately cover each jar with a lid and screw on a metal ring to hold the lid in place during the canning process.

The timing will vary based on the ingredients and equipment you are using. Once you have boiled or steamed your filled jars, promptly and carefully remove them from the boiling water and place them back on the towel-lined countertop to cool.

As the jars cool you will begin to hear a popping sound from time to time; this is the jar sealing. It can take up to 12 hours for jars to seal; you can assist in this process by pressing down on the middle of the lid with your finger, but if the lid does not remain concave it is a faulty seal. If the jars fail to seal, you should re-process the preserves. Depending on the brand of canning pot that you use, the guidelines differ slightly, so be sure to follow the manufacturer's instructions.

Once fully sealed, remove the rings for long-term storage; they are necessary only to hold the lids in place during processing and then again after you open the jar to use the contents. If left on during storage it becomes harder to detect a faulty seal, and the rings can also hold moisture from the canning process and cause rust to form around the edges.

NOTES ON INGREDIENTS

BUTTER Unless otherwise specified, all recipes use unsalted butter.

CALCIUM HYDROXIDE Also known as pickling lime. It is seasonally available in grocery stores and always obtainable online.

CITRIC ACID Be sure to buy food-grade crystals, which are readily available online.

DRIED ANGELINO PLUMS These plums, available online, are a vibrant shade of red. Regular dried plums or apricots can be substituted for a slightly different taste.

DRIED CHILES We favor Mexican chiles, such as ancho, guajillo, and chile de árbol, which range in flavor from mild to hot. These chiles are widely available at Latino markets and online.

FLOUR We like to use various types of flour to heighten flavor and yield interesting texture. In addition to wheat flours, including unbleached all-purpose, whole wheat, and spelt, buckwheat flour is used in one recipe. We try to use locally milled flours when possible; otherwise, Bob's Red Mill has a good selection in most grocery stores and also online at bobsredmill.com.

FLOWER PETALS Fresh rose petals must come from a fragrant variety that hasn't been treated with pesticides. If you don't have a gardener friend growing heirloom roses, fresh petals are available online from gourmetsweetbotanicals .com. Dried rose petals and orange blossoms can be substituted, as noted in the recipes. Both are available online.

HONEY Raw, unpasteurized honey is always our first choice, since it retains the healthful properties that are lost when heated. Granulated honey is honey that has been dried and milled into crystals that easily dissolve. It is available online.

MAPLE SYRUP We prefer dark grade B syrup for its rich flavor.

SALT We use Diamond Crystal kosher salt in our recipes.

SORGHUM SYRUP Processed from sorghum grain, this syrup is less viscous and slightly less sweet than molasses, a byproduct of sugar refining.

SUGAR Some recipes call for sucanat, which is unrefined cane sugar. White granulated sugar can be used in its place, though it will taste sweeter. We also like to use muscovado sugar, another type of unrefined cane sugar with a lovely toffee flavor.

VEGETABLE OILS Several recipes call for a neutral vegetable oil. We're partial to grapeseed oil, but a mild sunflower or peanut oil can be used instead. Unless it is specified, olive oil has too distinctive a flavor for most of our recipes.

VINEGAR We use many different types of vinegar, which vary from mild to bold. The gentlest is rice vinegar, which should be unseasoned. For apple cider vinegar, we prefer Bragg organic vinegar. We also use white wine, red wine, and champagne vinegars.

NOTES ON EQUIPMENT

BLENDERS Countertop and immersion blenders are put to use in many of the recipes in this book. In some cases, a food processor can be substituted, though blenders can be more effective for puréeing and pulsing certain ingredients.

CANDY THERMOMETER Candy thermometers measure the temperature of syrups, oils, and boiling sugar. These long-pronged thermometers can withstand higher heat than a meat thermometer, usually up to 400°F/200°C. Analog thermometers with clips that attach to the side of the pan and clearly marked stages of candy making are best.

CANNING JARS Many preservation recipes require a 1-pint/½ L glass canning jar with a metal lid for pickling, fermentation, and storage. It can be handy to have ½-pint or 2 pint jars as well. It's best to stock up on these before starting projects; packages of 6, 12, and 24 jars are usually available.

CHEESECLOTH Used for straining as well as to aerate during fermentation, cheesecloth is essential to have on hand for preservation recipes.

DEHYDRATOR A countertop dehydrator frees up oven or smart-oven space, especially when a recipe calls for 24 hours of slow drying at a very low temperature. Many models come fitted with special trays for dehydrating fruits, vegetables, and herbs.

FERMENTATION CROCKS While jars and glass bowls will usually suffice, contemporary crocks come specially designed for fermenting cabbage and other vegetables and fruits, and can include accessories such as weights and tampers. Korean earthenware crocks, known as *onggi*, are more traditional and are often decorative as well.

FERMENTATION WEIGHTS Glass fermentation weights are used to keep fruits and vegetables submerged in liquids. Substitutes include a clean stone, a small glass dish, or a zip-top bag filled with water.

FINE-MESH SIEVE A well-made, fine-mesh sieve is essential for straining, especially when a recipe calls for pressing on solids to extract liquid.

FOOD PROCESSOR For recipes that call for shredding, pulsing, and grinding, it pays to have a good food processor within reach, especially one with multiple blade options. A processor can also be used in place of a blender when necessary.

HEAVY-BOTTOMED, NONREACTIVE PANS Some preservation recipes call for a long, slow simmer. A sturdy stainless-steel pan will keep vegetables and fruits from scorching.

KITCHEN SCALE As with baking, preservation recipes work best when recipe amounts are strictly followed. Weighing ingredients on a kitchen scale ensures consistency.

PARCHMENT PAPER This smooth, greaseproof paper, known for its use in baking and cooking, also plays a key part in preservation recipes that call for fermenting in a jar or crock. Placed directly on top of the ingredients, it will prevent any stray bits from floating to the top.

SPICE GRINDER Because many of our recipes require grinding whole spices, this affordable countertop device is a great time-saver. Grinding by hand in a mortar and pestle is more old-school but completely acceptable.

WIRE COOLING RACK This kind of rack is a must for allowing air to circulate under baked goods as they cool and for draining fruits that have been cooked in syrup.

INDEX

ACKNOWLEDGMENTS

DARRA GOLDSTEIN

Thanks first to Cortney and Richard, my friends and coauthors. We enjoyed a dream team for this series, helmed by our visionary editor, Jenny Wapner, with whom it's always a joy to work. I'm also thrilled to be working again with another dear friend, designer Frances Baca, who has brought the books to such vivid life. It was great fun working with photographer David Malosh, whose gorgeous photos grace these books, and prop stylist Ayesha Patel. Thanks, too, to my agent, Angela Miller, and to Carolyn Insley for guiding the books through production. And finally I'm grateful for the unfailing support of my sister, Ardath Weaver, and that of my husband, Dean Crawford—for his math genius, his editing, and his endless enthusiasm for new tastes.

CORTNEY BURNS

In gratitude for the time honored preservation traditions that inspire and enliven our creativity. Thanks to my family for putting up with the plethora of jars and experiments that line our kitchen, and for tasting new and different flavors with wonderment and surprise. To my amazing collaboration team, Darra & Richard; what fun it is to create with you both. And to all the microbes that make this possible; we humbly thank you!

RICHARD MARTIN

I would like to thank my wife, Sonja, and children Apolline and Loic, for taste testing and allowing my food preservation experiments to take over the kitchen for long stretches of time. Thanks also to my extended family: Jan and John, Lee and Lisa, and Greg and Patty. Over the years, as a website and magazine editor, I've worked with many inspiring chefs, writers, and friends who expanded my culinary world—thanks to all of you. And to Darra and Cortney, thank you for developing these incredible recipes and allowing us to share them with the world.

The authors wish to thank Driscoll's and its farmers for sourcing green strawberries in the middle of winter.

Hardie Grant North America
2912 Telegraph Ave
Berkeley, CA 94705
hardiegrantbooks.com

Published in the United States by Hardie Grant North America,
an imprint of Hardie Grant Publishing Pty Ltd.

Library of Congress Cataloging-in-Publication Data is available
upon request

ISBN: 9781958417119
ISBN: 9781958417126 (eBook)

Printed in China
Design by Frances Baca
Prop styling by Ayesha Patel

FIRST EDITION

Hardie Grant

NORTH AMERICA

ABOUT THE AUTHORS

DARRA GOLDSTEIN the founding editor of *Gastronomica*, is the author of six award-winning cookbooks, including *Beyond the North Wind: Russia in Recipes and Lore,* named one of 2020's best cookbooks by *Forbes.com, Esquire*, and the *Washington Post*. In 2020 she was honored with the Lifetime Achievement Award from the International Association of Culinary Professionals.

CORTNEY BURNS (with chef Nick Balla) built a larder-based kitchen at San Francisco's Bar Tartine; their cookbook *Bar Tartine* won awards from both the James Beard Foundation and IACP. *Bon Appétit* has dubbed her the "godmother of fermentation" for her modern take on ancient techniques.

RICHARD MARTIN is a media executive, lifestyle editor, and writer who started magazines and websites that have grown into major media companies, including *Complex, Modern Luxury* (Manhattan and Miami), and *Food Republic*.